STRONG IN THE RAIN

KENJI MIYAZAWA

宮沢賢治

STRONG IN THE RAIN
SELECTED POEMS

TRANSLATED BY ROGER PULVERS

BLOODAXE BOOKS

ISBN: 978 1 85224 781 2

First published 2007 by
Bloodaxe Books Ltd,
Eastburn,
South Park,
Hexham,
Northumberland NE46 1BS.

www.bloodaxebooks.com
For further information about Bloodaxe titles
please visit our website or write to
the above address for a catalogue.

Supported using public funding by
**ARTS COUNCIL
ENGLAND**

This book has been selected by the Japanese Publishing Project (JLPP)
which is run by the Japanese Literature Publishing and Promotion Center
(J-Lit Center) on behalf of the Agency for Cultural Affairs of Japan.

Cover design: Neil Astley & Pamela Robertson-Pearce.

Digital reprint of the 2007 Bloodaxe Books edition.

These translations are for my wife, Susan
and our children
Jeremy, Alice, Sophie and Lucy
all of whom are bilingual in Japanese and English

CONTENTS

INTRODUCTION

Kenji Miyazawa drew on nature in a way that no other modern Japanese author had before him. He observed, absorbed and re-created it, without resorting to fashioned counterworking or the traditional artifice of lament.

In the introduction to his collection of short stories, *The Restaurant of Many Orders*, he clearly sees himself as a medium for the reprocessing of nature: that is, natural phenomena of light, wind and rain are processed through him before they are recreated on the page.

'These stories of mine,' he wrote, 'all came to me from moonlight and rainbows, in places like railroad tracks and fields and forests.'

As a writer and poet of the *plein air* variety, he trekked from the rolling farmland and the marshes to the mountains of his native Iwate, making what he termed 'mental sketches modified'.

Then he went one step further and pictured himself, in 'Preface to *Spring and Ashura*', in terms of light.

The phenomenon called I
Is a single blue illumination
Of a presupposed organic alternating current lamp
    (a composite body of each and every transparent spectre)
The single illumination
Of karma's alternating current lamp
Remains alight without fail
Flickering unceasingly, restlessly
Together with the sights of the land and all else
    (the light is preserved...the lamp itself is lost)

Not content to sit on the sidelines squinting and sighing with resignation, Kenji threw himself into nature. He could not separate himself from what he observed, and he believed that it was his duty to teach others to take robust action out of religious conviction.

(In this book I refer to the poet by his given name, Kenji. It is the custom in Japan to call famous writers and poets by their first name, though this is not always the case. Yukio Mishima is never referred to as 'Yukio', nor is Yasunari Kawabata called 'Yasunari'. Poets Takuboku and Kenji, and novelists Soseki and Ogai – all of these are given names – are referred to in this way.)

This active engagement with nature, and his seeing himself as its faithful chronicler and recorder, was sufficient to set him apart from virtually all other Japanese poets, who tended to use nature as a springboard for their own musings and lamentations. Because of this characteristic, if no other, he suffered the fate of being the most misunderstood Japanese literary figure of the 20th century.

In the mid-1990s, however, as if to redress the balance, the work of Kenji Miyazawa received unprecedented attention in the Japanese media. Hardly a day went by at that time when he was not featured in a national newspaper or magazine, or discussed on radio or television. (Japan had fallen into its worst recession of the postwar period, and young people were beginning to question the goal of economic expansion for its own sake. In this context, the alternative system of values underlying Kenji's work – being close to nature and acting on the basis of compassion and empathy – was attractive to many.)

In the first half of 1996 alone, three lengthy television docudramas were made about his life and writing, and two feature films went into production.

No author, living or dead, had ever received such concentrated attention. Kenji Miyazawa himself, more than sixty years after his death, had miraculously come up in the world, seen himself hauled up rank by rank in the literary states of existence from somewhere in semi-honorary literary limbo to heights of esteem bordering on adulation.

What was behind this turnabout? Was Kenji Miyazawa being made into a saint, a 'holy man from Hanamaki'? Was this boom genuine – a true interest held by the reading public and reflected properly in the media?

A Rare Exception

During Kenji's lifetime (1896–1933), the people of Iwate Prefecture in Tohoku (the northern prefectures on the main island of Honshu) struggled to subsist. The development of Japan has always been radically uneven. In the Japan of the Meiji Era (1868–1912), wealth gravitated to the major port cities that emerged from feudalistic practices, both civic and economic. The country was settling, not without considerable social upheaval, into the customs of modernisation. People in the large port cities realised that it was often necessary to replace traditional feudalistic relationships in the workplace and elsewhere with Western mores and ways of thinking.

The farmers in many rural areas, however, found themselves pushed behind. Their traditional social organisations did not always prepare them well for scientific farming; and, as in the case of Iwate, their lack of easy access to international ports such as Yokohama and Kobe, from which the Kanto and Kansai regions drew their bounty, prevented them from acquiring either the means or the information necessary to keep apace.

Destitution sent men from the Tohoku area primarily to Tokyo, whose gateway for them was Ueno. Young girls, too, were sent away to spinning mills, if they were lucky. It is said that the wooden *kokeshi* dolls, popular in the northern prefectures of Honshu, were effigies of affection kept by parents and grandparents to remind them of their lost little girls.

Kenji Miyazawa was a rare exception. Born in Hanamaki as the eldest of five children into a well-off family – his father was the town pawnbroker – Kenji was obliged to watch at close hand while the miserable tenant farmers of the district traded their meagre personal goods for a pittance. (Pawnbrokering, particularly in rural Japan, where banking facilities were not as sophisticated as in the major cities like Tokyo, Yokohama, Osaka, or Kobe, was not a disrespectful vocation. Kenji's father, Masajiro, was a pillar of the Hanamaki community, and pawnbrokers like him were seen as providing necessary services to farmers in need of cash to tide them over during years of poor harvest or drought.)

By rights the eldest son should have continued in his father's footsteps. Even in a Japan bent on militarising, eldest sons were exempt from conscription. Following dutifully in the family line was considered that important. Refusing to do so was a dramatic act of rebellion.

I cannot help but think that Kenji must have suffered more than a few pangs of conscience, viewing poor farmers shuffling in and out of his father's pawnshop. He would have to find a way to do something on these people's behalf, to prove to them that he cared personally about their lot.

When Kenji turned into an extremely devout – some would say 'fanatical' – follower of the Nichiren sect of Buddhism, he tried in vain to convert his father, who was a dedicated follower of the Jodo Shinshu sect and had in fact been instrumental in founding the Hanamaki Buddhist Society. As a result, the relationship between father and son deteriorated badly (though Kenji seemed reluctant to reject his father's money, which enabled him to travel, study and proselytise). Yet it seems to me that the core of the lifelong feud was not based on doctrinal conviction, but rather on a funda-mental personality clash of the most ordinary type between father and son. Neither would accept each other for what they were: the father, a narrow-minded patriarch who lent money to the poor in exchange for their property or pledges; the son, an equally narrow-minded rebel with a cause, positively determined to sacrifice himself for the happiness of others.

And the two men were bound by more than such typical antipathy. It seemed that illness united them as well. Kenji underwent an operation on his nose at the Iwate Hospital in Morioka while in middle school. On a visit to see Kenji in the hospital, his father caught the infection that Kenji had apparently developed post-operatively.

In more superstitious times one might assume that Kenji was willing his father to take notice of the human state of the wretched, ill and unfortunate. Of course there was a medical explanation for it, but nonetheless it must have occurred to both men that their fates were intertwined in more ways than one.

An Act of Ego

Japan's victory in the Russo-Japanese War in 1905 sent waves of patriotic sentiment across the country. Japan was well into the process of colonising Korea, which it would annex by force in 1910. Most clever young men with a social conscience – and Kenji's social conscience burned incessantly inside him – would turn primarily to either commerce or the military as the outlet for their gifts.

As he went through school, however, Kenji took an increasing interest in plants and minerals. Had he been born and raised in Tokyo or Kyoto, for instance, he might have gone on to graduate school and a career in the natural sciences, either biology or geology. As it was, he opted for agronomy, keeping biology, geology, and later, astronomy as intellectual pastimes.

In fact, he dabbled in many disciplines: he studied English, German and Esperanto, and had an abiding love of classical music, which he played at great length on his cello or his gramophone to what must have been a somewhat bewildered audience of visitors and pupils.

Picture him teaching young people at the Las Chijin Association, which he established in his house by the side of a field in Hanamaki, pacing in front of his students and bashing their ears about the genius of Ludwig Zamenhof, the Polish-Jewish oculist who founded Esperanto; or rehearsing them in one of his morality plays; or preaching to them about the joys of vegetarianism at a time when some of them would have been thrilled to see the occasional fillet of a dried sardine on their plate. (The word 'las' in the Las Chijin Association is Polish, and means 'forest'; 'Chijin' means 'people of the earth'.)

The stories that are told of Kenji refusing food given to him by his parents, of even throwing it ostentatiously down a well, and of sitting down with a friend and virtually forcefeeding him a pile of tomatoes, are probably quite true. To Kenji, even eating came to be seen as an act of ego. Like the Russian writer Nikolai Gogol, his purpose in life and the primary inspiration behind his writing came to be his religious fanaticism; and like Gogol, Kenji may be said to have starved himself to death, or at least to have exacerbated his tubercular condition.

There were two main themes, then, in his life, both related to guilt: that acquired at his father's pawnshop, and that born of the inner need to instruct and convince others. Taken together, they formed an ideology of self-sacrifice that eventually destroyed his body, while creating a spiritual legacy that took more than half a century to come to light. There is no doubt that the major personal event in Kenji Miyazawa's life was the death of his little sister, Toshi (or Toshiko).

Kenji, it must be remembered, was a man who displayed no particular interest in romantic love or sex. He is, I think, the only major Japanese author, certainly in the modern era, whose works make no reference whatsoever to sex and only scant mention of love of the heart between two adults.

He never married, but he certainly could have, coming from such a well-to-do family and having a respected career as a teacher. Offers of arranged marriage were, indeed, made to him at least twice. But he saw himself as too frail and sickly to take on the responsibility of a wife and family. It was a distraction he could ill afford. He lived most of his adult life alone.

Kenji and his sister were very close, as was attested to me in private conversations with their brother, Seiroku. After Toshi died of tuberculosis at 24 (Kenji was two years older), he composed three of his most famous poems, subsequently dating them to the very day of her death. One of them, 'The Morning of Last Farewell' (see page 79), begins...

O my little sister
Who will travel far on this day
It is sleeting outside and strangely light

How could he come to terms with it, if not by accepting it as a mere passing from one state to another, as not an ending but instead a single small step through the Buddhist realms of existence.

The sleet sloshes down, sinking
Out of sombre clouds the colour of bismuth

13

O Toshiko!
You asked me for a bowl
Of this refreshing snow
When you were on the point of death
To brighten my life forever
Thank you my brave little sister
I too will not waver from my path

The next year he took a ship to the southern part of Sakhalin, the large island directly north of Hokkaido, at the time a Japanese possession. I am convinced that in his mind the purpose of his trip was not to forget Toshi, but to go in search of her. The poems he wrote about this trip are essentially about Toshi and a way to communicate with her spirit through the natural phenomena that he saw on the trip while travelling.

If Kenji thought he might come to understand the real and natural state of the dead spirit on the cold waters of the Sea of Okhotsk, he imagined that state in fiction a few years later when he wrote his classic novel, *Night on the Milky Way Train*.

Part of the River Itself

The lovely story running through this novel is a parable. It describes the dream of a boy, Giovanni, as he takes a ride in a railway car throughout the heavens in the company of his best friend, Campanella. Kenji gave Italian names, the latter more a family name than a first, to his two heroes. There are characters in the story with Japanese names as well, but it is clear from the line of the narration that this is a tale of universal setting in more ways than one.

The two boys, meeting up with eccentric and fascinating people who inhabit or are passing through the sky on their way to their individual destinations, travel throughout the galaxy, from one constellation to another.

Giovanni is never quite sure where the train is heading, and is surprised, when asked by the conductor for his ticket, to find a small folded piece of paper in his pocket. The two boys gaze at the ticket in amazement, feeling that 'if they continued to stare at it they would certainly be swallowed up into it'.

'Good heavens,' says the birdcatcher, a crusty character who catches herons in the Milky Way and presses them into cakes that are as good as goose. 'That ticket is really tops. It will take you higher than the sky. With this ticket you've got safe conduct to anywhere your heart desires to go. With this ticket you can go wherever you wish on the imperfect Four-Dimensional-Milky-Way-Dream Train.'

14

'Giovanni's Ticket' is the last and longest chapter of *Night on the Milky Way Train*. For Kenji, the little piece of folded green paper which miraculously appeared out of Giovanni's pocket is a pass to another world, and back.

In a flash Campanella is gone from the train. Giovanni feels abandoned: after all, weren't the two friends going to continue on and on to the ends of the earth and beyond? Giovanni wakes up in the grass on the hill overlooking his town, where a festival is in progress. He makes his way down to the river. He is told that a boy has fallen in and has not been found. It is, of course, Campanella. Campanella actually jumped into the water to save another boy, who was, earlier in the story, not very nice to him.

The startling thing about the ending is, to me, Campanella's father's attitude in the face of his son's death. After only 45 minutes he decides to accept the fact. While gripping his watch tightly in his fist, he politely asks after Giovanni's father, who is due to return home after a stint up north at the government's pleasure. He invites Giovanni to his home the next day, when the other children will be paying a visit for what will probably be a wake.

> With those words Campanella's father gazed far downstream, where the galaxy was part of the river itself.

Kenji is calming himself over the death of his sister, telling himself that it is precisely at times of profound sadness that people should think not of the dead or of themselves, but rather of the welfare of others.

By the end, Giovanni has resigned himself to his friend's fate.

> Downstream, the Milky Way was reflected from one edge of the river to the other as if there were no water there at all but only sky.
>
> Giovanni felt that by now Campanella could be nowhere but on the very farthest edge of that river of the sky.

Solitary Boy

Kenji's position in modern Japanese literature is unique. There have been many writers who have emulated the style of Ogai Mori (Yukio Mishima being the most notable), Soseki Natsume, Ichiyo Higuchi, Takuboku Ishikawa, Akiko Yosano and other great novelists and poets, but no one is able to reproduce, in style or spirit, the Japanese of Kenji Miyazawa. Where does his immense imagination, in terms of both content and style, come from? The answer to this question lies, no doubt, in his childhood.

Kenji wrote many of his stories not only about children, but as seen from the standpoint, and with the perspective, of children.

Many of the heroes of his stories are lonely little boys. Judging from Kenji's own life as a misunderstood and lonely person, I believe that it is correct to see these boys as recreations of his own life.

When I think of Kenji as a little boy, his story 'The Fourth Day of Narcissus' comes to mind. (In this title, the flower, the narcissus, is being used as if it were the name of a month. Kenji named a month after this flower without saying what month he imagined the story taking place; but it is likely February, as the narcissus is the harbinger of spring.)

> A solitary boy wrapped in a red blanket cape was bustling along the foot of a snow hill in the shape of a huge elephant's head, and as he hurried home all he could think about was hot caramel.

This solitary boy encounters a Snow Child, who is, perhaps, his double. The child sings two little ditties to the stars in a loud voice. The child implores Cassiopeia to spin her glass waterwheel with a squeaky noise. He asks Andromeda to burn its alcohol lamp until it hisses.

When he was a boy, Kenji's hobby was collecting rocks. But he was also fascinated by the stars. And like the little boy in 'The Fourth Day of Narcissus' and the children in other stories of his, he could see animals and plants that others, especially adults, could not see.

Later, when he became a writer, he retained this outlook and insight, and he interpreted the world of people, nature and all things around him in terms of them. That is to say, his imagination was his real world, and whatever he observed and studied was interpreted in terms of it. Kenji Miyazawa is not a writer of fantasies. Many critics and readers alike have categorised his work as fantasy, or children's, literature. Of course, there is nothing wrong with these categories. They simply do not apply to Kenji. What he saw was totally real to him – be it a Snow Wolf that is whipped up by the wind or a constellation of stars that makes music. He did not conjure up these images to entertain or delight readers. He described what he saw in order to teach people the truth of the nature of the world.

As a little boy, Kenji sought escape. But there was not much entertainment in Hanamaki at the time. (The first cinema in the district, the Kinenkan, was opened in 1916 in nearby Morioka. As an adult, Kenji spent more than a year in Tokyo, spreading the religious message and striving to get converts for Kokuchukai. In his free time, he loved to visit the entertainment areas of Asakusa, especially the cinema there.) He certainly considered himself different from the people around him, but he was close to his mother and his little sister Toshi. He was an extremely energetic child who, like a lot of the boys in his stories, could not stay still, and who always wanted to study something new, be involved in any adventure, even if it was just to walk the mountains, particularly Mount Iwate. In adulthood, due to this craving for activity, he dipped into all sorts of pursuits and hobbies: music appreciation, Esperanto, philosophy and geology, among many others. Writing stories and poetry was one of those creative pursuits, though I do believe that he considered himself a writer above all else and, like other authors, was very ambitious. He wanted his work to be published and widely read, though in his case the primary motivation was to convert readers to the faith of Nichiren Buddhism.

As was mentioned, his relationship with his father was strained, to say the least. Masajiro did not approve of most of the life decisions that Kenji made for himself, and he tried to prevent his son from going into a few professions, including the handcrafted jewellery business that might actually have suited Kenji quite well.

It wasn't until 1920, when he was already 24, that Kenji converted to the Nichiren sect and joined the ultranationalist Kokuchukai society (meaning, literally, 'National Pillar Society'). This group was founded in the 1880s by the charismatic preacher and scholar Chigaku Tanaka. Kenji was attracted to the group's robust, aggressive proselytising philosophy. (He was naïve about political matters. He died in 1933, just as Japanese incursions on the Asian continent were beginning. Had he lived, he might well have supported the Japanese war effort.) Masajiro, who opposed Kenji's religious views outright and saw them as dogmatic, was not pleased about his son's conversion.

By 1922, when he was 26, Kenji was teaching at the Hanamaki Agricultural School. He had become a fully fledged teacher of science and a person who believed in the strictest methodologies of observing and recording natural phenomena. But all the while he was writing poems and stories that he published using his own money. (Self-publishing was very common at the time in Japan and the West, and was not considered shameful. James Joyce, D.H. Lawrence, and Anaïs Nin are all examples of writers who sometimes published their own works.)

Toshi died on 27 November 1922. Ultimately the psychological crisis that this plunged him into was assuaged by his absolute conviction that death was not final, that life itself was only the briefest state, an instant in the life of a spark, and that his beloved sister

17

had gone on to a better place. But the sadness that her death caused in him and his need personally to overcome it gave rise to a great tension inside him. I believe that his best poems and stories were written in the years following Toshi's death.

In 1926, Kenji left teaching. He had certainly thrown himself fully into that work, taking his students on excursions and field trips and sharing his wide knowledge of agronomy, particularly relating to the use of fertilisers. But teaching, curiously, had taken him away from the soil. It is generally thought that he desired to become a farmer himself and have a farmer's relationship with the land. But I do not believe this to be the whole story. His desire to farm may have been a rationalisation of his circumstances at the time.

Having lost his sister, and still largely estranged from his hard-headed father, Kenji felt more and more isolated in Hanamaki. In an era like ours today he might have gone to Europe or America to live. Instead he chose to retreat into farming and surround himself with his many intellectual and artistic interests. Why didn't he go back to Tokyo, though, where he had proselytised for the Kokuchukai? The answer to that, I think, lies in his personality. Kenji made few friends in Tokyo. Who could take a writer like him seriously in a Tokyo that had a myriad of sophisticated literary schools and pol-emical factions and magazines that served small coteries of avant-garde writers? The cultural elite of Tokyo was not concerned with fertilising rural Japan, as Kenji was, but with empire, industriali-sation, modernisation and militarising. Japan was looking outward, towards Manchuria, the rest of China and, eventually, all of Asia, which many Japanese wanted to see as part of Japan's great new empire. Where was the place in Tokyo for a fertiliser expert from Hanamaki who was living out the illusions of his imagination?

Despite what a few of his surviving students have said decades later, I do not believe that Kenji was a particularly popular teacher. He had a very difficult personality. Out of conviction and enthusi-asm, he wanted desperately for others to follow his example. He tried to convert people to his faith and to vegetarianism, a practice that has very few adherents even in today's Japan.

Kenji was too old – and too proud – by then to live in his par-ents' home. Now 30 and living alone, he took refuge in the com-panionship of the characters in his stories.

By the end of 1928 he fell ill again, with pneumonia. His lungs had been weakened by an earlier case of pleurisy. He had been gravely ill a number of times during his lifetime, and he had always had access to good medical care. But this time it certainly looked like the end, as we see in several poems, such as 'Speaking with the Eyes' (see page 46):

It's blue and still out there
It looks like death...and very soon at that

The Sanctity of Life

Kenji's poetry and fiction were rediscovered by the Japanese long after his death. I believe that readers in the rest of the world will likewise discover his work in our century. My belief in this stems from one of Kenji's own themes: the relationship between humans and animals.

There is perhaps no more vivid example of this than his story 'Snow Crossing'. But even so, 'Snow Crossing' is by no means unique among his works. Other stories that depict the interrelatedness of humans and animals are 'The Acorns and the Wildcat', 'Gauche the Cellist', 'The Bears of Mount Nametoko' and 'The Restaurant of Many Orders', though in this last example it is the hunters themselves who nearly end up in the 'hunters' stew'.

Kenji's stories are parables about the sanctity of life. In this he is not especially different from other writers. But he parts company with Western writers who depict animals among humans. To most Jews and Christians, humans are the highest form of life. Animals do not have souls. Buddhism, at least as an ideal, reveres all life on one plane. The soul of a human being can return in the body of an animal. A deep reverence for all life is an essential element of Buddhist theory.

There is interaction, of course, between humans and animals in traditional and modern Western tales, but this is rarely interaction on an equal level. Animals are, by and large, there to scare humans or serve them. In the stories popularised by Disney, the animals are often anthropomorphic. This means that they are really humans in animal skins, made to look cute or cruel to serve what is actually a story about human relations.

For Kenji, animals are either on the same level as humans, or higher. They may have been the victims of human caprice or design, and suffer because of it. They may just want to be friends. Bears talk among themselves; hawks chatter, as do wildcats, mice, cats and others. But this is not the cutesy conversation of Disney characters. If anything, Kenji's animals exhibit wisdom and resignation and sadness, conveying these to humans in order to enlighten them.

Kenji's message, as we see in his poetry too, is that all humans and animals are part of creation, and we must all live in harmony with each other or we will perish together. Kenji believes that children understand this better than adults, and that is why he has such strong affinities, at least on paper, with children.

At the end of 'Snow Crossing', after the foxes' magic lantern show, Konzaburo the fox says:

> There is something that you all must truly take to heart tonight. And that is the fact that two children of human beings, both clever and not in the least drunk, have been kind enough to eat food made by foxes. I believe that in the future you, as adults, will neither tell lies nor be envious of others...

These messages remain relevant for our century. We must realise the danger of viewing humans as the conquering heroes of nature. We must see ourselves as only one part of nature, a part that should not excessively manipulate and destroy nature for our own temporary gains. Kenji is constantly telling us that we must have the humility to understand that animals, too, have souls like us, and that it is perilous for us to close our eyes to this.

True Happiness

Kenji wrote in his best-known poem, 'Strong in the Rain' – the last poem in this collection – that the 'kind of person he wanted to be' was one called 'a blockhead' and never taken to heart. There are many lonely characters of this sort in his stories, but perhaps none who so closely resembles the author himself as Kenju in 'Kenju Park Woods'. While the written character used for 'Ken' in Kenju is different from the 'Ken' in Kenji, the fact that they are homonymic makes the identification fairly certain.

In this beautiful story about humans and nature, Kenju is exactly the kind of overlooked blockhead that Kenji wanted to be. Kenju is overjoyed by glimpses of nature:

> His eyes blinked and blinked in glee at the sight of the blue-green groves in the rain, he jumped for joy when he caught sight of a hawk flying up and up into the blue sky, and clapped his hands when he told everyone about it.

He was unable, though, to make the same connections with other children that he enjoyed with nature:

> But the other children jeered at Kenju so much that Kenju gradually pretended not to laugh.

Kenji, like Kenju in the story, derived most of the joy in his life not from his bonds with other people, but from his companionship with nature. If Kenji had a friend and a lover in life, it was nature.

But Japan, since the Meiji Era, had set headlong in the direction of industrialisation: a nation striving to accomplish in a generation or two what had taken Europe well over a century. The result was that the traditional Japanese love of and respect for nature was largely abandoned in practice but retained as a national myth. Most of Kenji's contemporaries would have believed – as Japanese still tend to believe today – that the Japanese love nature virtually more than do the people of any other nation. This belief is held despite the fact that preservation of nature is a very low priority for those people in Japan who hold the future of the country in their hands. Nature itself has become nothing more than a figment of nostalgia to most Japanese people.

Kenji, at his hometown so remote from the centre of power in the new Japan, was, I believe, as keenly aware as anyone of the cost that Japan was paying and would pay in the future for its new industrial might. Yet he was not a "back-to-nature" kind of romanticist. Kenji Miyazawa did not share the view of Japan that the country was better off in a state of blissful nature worship. Kenji was a scientist, not a mystic. His spiritual beliefs may have been dogmatic, but his view of the modern village was concrete and forward-looking.

Kenji believed that the Japanese people would die in spirit if they did not continue to recognise beauty and true happiness in nature. Humans, birds, insects and all other creatures pass on; it is the trees and the light and the wind that retain and carry their messages to future generations.

In 'Kenju Park Woods' there is an unscrupulous man named Heiji. This Heiji 'did do a little farming, but his real job was something else, something that people found offensive'.

> Kenju planted a cryptomeria wood and Heiji wanted him to cut the trees down.
> 'Cut 'em down, I say, cut 'em down, will ya!'
> Kenju stands his ground.
> 'No, I won't!' he says.
> And Heiji proceeds to beat the hell out of Kenju.

Later that year Heiji dies of typhus, and ten days later Kenju dies of the same disease. We may all share the same fate – even the same illness – whatever our beliefs and actions may be. In Kenji's Buddhist world, victim and victimiser are linked, like two mountain climbers connected by a rope on a high cliff in the snow. Being good does not save us. After all, Campanella was the one who died in the river.

The people in Kenju's village gradually began to accept their woods, however, giving names to its rows of trees: Tokyo Road, Russia Road, Road of the Occident. Even in the provincial outpost of Hanamaki, Kenji Miyazawa had a cosmopolitan view of the world. There is frequent mention of countries around the world in his poetry and prose, and only rarely does he mention Japan. You don't need to travel the world and be a connoisseur of wines to be a cosmopolitan. You don't have to mention your country over and over again to love what it stands for.

In the story, Kenju's wisdom is acknowledged years later. But it is the continued presence of the trees, the very spirit of Kenju himself, that stands as a source of true happiness for the people.

Kenji believed deeply in the Ten Powers of a Buddha and wished to acquire these powers himself. (After all, the 'ju' in Kenju is ten.) Of these Ten Powers, perhaps the one that he most wanted all of us to gain is the first: the power of knowing what is true and what is not.

Someone who sees the truth in one era may be branded a fool by his contemporaries. But that same fool may prove, in the future, to be a prophet. For Kenji, the future is contained in the past and the present. There is no need to "foresee". There is only a need to know, recognise, and accept.

Kenji believed that true happiness comes to humans from nature. This faith helped him to overcome his fears of illness and death.

> On days like that, when the rain just flowed down from a soft pure-white sky, Kenju would stand outside the woods all alone, getting soaked to the bone.

The portrait of Kenju is a self-portrait of Kenji similar to the one in 'Whatever Anyone Says' (see page 50). He is now a tree, dripping with dew.

'Such Is the Power of My Wisdom'

The element in Kenji Miyazawa's life and work that is perhaps most difficult for us to understand today is his religious fervour. Japanese today are generally not religious in the same way that he was. The vast majority of Japanese people, when surveyed, describe themselves as areligious. Among those who actively identify themselves as adhering to the Buddhist faith, most, again, are not keen on proselytising. (The Nichiren sect, to which Kenji pledged his loyalty, is an exception.)

There are quite a few poems written on an openly religious theme, such as 'An Icy Joke' (see page 85). But when it comes to his stories, religious themes permeate virtually all of them. The very first Kenji story that I read, back in 1968, was 'The Story of the Zashiki Bokko', a prose poem included in this collection (see page 55). Here it is obvious that some strange things are occurring in the household when a little boy appears (and yet at the same time is not there) and eerie sounds are heard in empty rooms. These phenomena are often brought on by the wind – a force that Kenji personified in his famous story, 'Matasaburo of the Wind'. His stories often feature a sick child, or a child who is about to die.

One of Kenji's most deeply religious stories is 'Bare Feet of Light'. It treats the subject of faith so nakedly that Kenji himself, in a note written on the manuscript in red ink, labelled it 'sentimental'. In a sense, 'Bare Feet of Light' is a continuation of the journey of the Milky Way Train. Ichiro in 'Bare Feet of Light' accompanies his little brother, Narao, to the other world, but is sent back to this one to finish his life as a human, thanks to his good deed of trying to protect Narao from the harsh cold of the snow.

'Bare Feet of Light' is about sacrifice and death, goodness and evil, and the eventual salvation of the soul.

Kenji may be at his best as a stylist when he describes light, wind, and snow. Some of the passages in 'Bare Feet of Light' are among his most lyrical and exquisite. In the beginning, the two brothers are visiting their father in the mountains. Their father is making charcoal to sell during the winter. The hut that they are staying in is filled with smoke and blue light (in Kenji's work, blue light is often a portent of death.) Narao begins to think of something else, something hazy and beyond him. This is Kenji's way of telling us that Narao is envisioning death: his own. (Using similar language, Giovanni also foresees Campanella's death in *Night on the Milky Way Train*, though he is not able to pinpoint the reason for his sadness.)

It is important, when translating literature, to understand the meaning behind ambiguous expressions, have a clear image of the range of what they could mean, decide on the correct interpretation of the ambiguity, and then find a similarly ambiguous or vague phrase in one's own language to use for the translation. This is particularly difficult when translating Kenji Miyazawa, because he uses a good deal of strangely ambiguous and sometimes downright bizarre Japanese. This style must not be made to sound bland and ordinary in English.

Let's take a look at a beautiful passage from 'Bare Feet of Light'.

The sky was slippery, as if polished by blue light and the boys' eyes tingled, smarting from the light. One look at the sun, and it appeared like a gigantic gemstone in the sky, scattering green and bitter orange and droplets of brightness, and when they shut their eyes because of the intense glare, the gem just looked bluer than blue in the blue-black dark, and when they opened them again, countless shadows of the sun were swimming and trembling before them, golden and dark-violet against the same blue sky.

This is a story about light, because it is the light of the World-Honoured One that turns hell into paradise and evil into good. The World-Honoured One tells the boys:

> There is nothing to be frightened of. Compared to the great virtue that envelopes the world, your sins are what a little drop of dew on the point of a thistle's thorn is to the light of the sun.

For Kenji, however dark human suffering may be, it is only a speck in a vast universe of healing and light.

That place where Kenji sends his characters who pass away is like a museum. It is a museum where all reality is stored. Everything we do – good, bad, or indifferent – is recorded there. When we die, we will be held accountable for these actions, and for everything done by our ancestors. This is the key to Kenji's morality. He is convinced that this is what is awaiting all of us, and he wants so desperately for us to be convinced as well.

Kenji first read the Lotus Sutra when he was a teenager. Later, in 'Bare Feet of Light', he referred to Book 16 of this sutra. Towards the end of Book 16, the World-Honoured One states, in the form of verse...

> Such is the power of my wisdom
> That its sagacious beams shine without bound

And at the very end, the World-Honoured One proclaims:

> How can I cause living beings
> To gain entry into the Unsurpassed Way
> And quickly acquire the body of Buddha?

This is exactly how Kenji viewed his own personal mission. He wanted to help others become enlightened. By doing this, through self-sacrifice, he would gain his own entry into paradise.

The Chosen Few

Of all Japanese writers of the 20th century (the century in which the world "discovered" Japanese literature) Kenji Miyazawa should have been translated, read, and recognised in the West. Alas, it did not happen.

Why was Kenji neglected? The reasons can be attributed to both Japan and the West.

Japan was slow to recognise this poet and storyteller of genius. For one thing, Kenji was classified by critics as a "fantasy writer for children". Certainly many of Kenji's stories are about children. It can also be said that some of his stories are written in a child-like style. (His poems, however, are hardly for children. They are hard enough for adults to read!)

But as was mentioned, I have always believed that Kenji Miyazawa's work is not "fantasy". The events and descriptions in his stories are not illusions; they are faithful descriptions of what he saw and felt at the time, and they appear in his narratives for specific purposes, chiefly of religious allegory. The bulk of Kenji's fiction is parable.

Another reason for the lack of recognition in Japan for Kenji's literature stems from the fact that he was very much a local writer, whose dialect and stylistic rhythms were considerably different from what critics and literary editors had come to think of as "modern". There have been, needless to say, other major writers from Tohoku, including the haiku poet Takuboku Ishikawa, whose work directly inspired Kenji; the novelist Osamu Dazai, known as a "decadent" writer in the immediate postwar years; the satirical essayist and fiction writer Ango Sakaguchi (who was actually from nearby Niigata, technically in Hokuriku, not Tohoku), and even, in our day, Shuji Terayama, a playwright, poet, and essayist who has been influencing young people since the 1960s. But all of these writers adapted their style to suit Tokyo's – the nation's – taste, and there is scant use of dialect in their works. Publishers and editors were often simply unable to fathom Kenji's literary language, with its dialect, religious message, and esoteric scientific references.

Finally, I believe that Kenji Miyazawa's deeply religious themes have been an obstacle to his gaining acceptance among the general Japanese reading public as an author who is representative of Japan. There are other authors who have been greatly inspired by Buddhism, from Kyoka Izumi and Yukio Mishima to Jakucho Setouchi, just to name a few. But Buddhism for them is a philosophical backdrop – even for Setouchi, who became a Buddhist nun. For Kenji it is central – both medium and message, core and essence. Kenji's convictions are not part of the mainstream of Japanese Buddhism. Buddhism in Japan today has been largely relegated to the role of just one of many influences on behaviour, together with Confucianism, Shinto, and others.

Japan is a country where great writers are often given ample recognition and fame in their lifetime. If anything, they are lionised and obliged by editors and publishers to write too much, to spread themselves too thinly.

The reasons behind the Kenji boom of the 1990s were less literary than social. The recession caused Japanese people to reflect on the various ills of Japanese society, including those that were primarily economic in origin, such as exorbitant prices for land and rampant consumerism; those that were political, like corruption and neglect of people's real needs; and social ills like child abuse, poverty and homelessness. Kenji Miyazawa was one writer who cared deeply and personally about individual welfare and happiness. He preached – and preached is the proper word for it – that every individual should make sacrifices as a matter of individual conscience. This seemed to be a positive and helpful message for a Japan that was slipping into a lost decade. The bubble economy had collapsed by 1993. Japanese companies that had promised lifetime employment were now sacking workers. Issues of domestic violence, child abuse, and bullying were dominating the media. In January 1995, large sections of the city of Kobe and the surrounding districts were destroyed by a massive earthquake, killing more than six thousand people. This was followed by the sarin gas attack on the Tokyo subways, perpetrated by a fanatical religious sect called Aum Shinrikyo. Japan's confidence as a safe, ever-prosperous country was shattered. Many young people could no longer believe in the Japanese way of life as it was presented to them by the older generations. Kenji's philosophy of active, personal sacrifice for others – helping each individual one by one – seemed to be an answer to what was lacking in Japan.

There are several reasons for Kenji Miyazawa not being discovered in the West.

The neglect in Japan is one of them. Until the 1980s, the influence of the Japanese literary establishment, or *bundan*, on which authors were considered worthy of introduction to the West was considerable. The literature of Junichiro Tanizaki, Yasunari Kawabata, and Yukio Mishima, to name three, was chosen as being expressive of the "Japanese sensibility". The West has long entertained a rarefied notion of Japaneseness, and sought in Japan the sensitive, the sensual, and the serene.

Since the end of the 20th century, however, there has been a marked decline in interest in the West in the kinds of Japanese novels that are seen to be "typically Japanese". (I put this in quotation-marks because I don't believe the work of any author to be typically Japanese. An author only represents one small segment of a world that he or she imagines.) There appeared a genuine interest all around the world in works by such contemporary authors as Haruki Murakami and Banana Yoshimoto. These writers are not seen in the West as being particularly Japanese in style or content. It is the absence of "Japanese" elements, combined with the universal alienation of the characters in the novels and stories of these authors, that has primarily appealed to non-Japanese readers around the world.

Kenji Miyazawa was not one of the chosen few destined to be "representative" either of the older school of Japaneseness or the contemporary one of universal alienation.

Supernova

In order to understand why Kenji Miyazawa's popularity suddenly grew, as if he were the light from a supernova that exploded years before the light reached the earth, one must view him in terms of his times and location.

He was fiercely committed to bringing rural Hanamaki up to the level of the more developed regions of Japan. His letters to friends contain detailed scientific information on the use of fertilisers. Several of the last hours of his life, during which he was in considerable pain, were apparently spent in lively discussion with a local farmer about how the man's crop could be improved. As an agronomist, when he believed that his own advice had been insufficient, he had gone around giving parcels of money to those farmers he had failed to help.

His faith was placed squarely in the consciousness of each and every individual. In 'Outline of an Introduction to Agrarian Art', written in verse form, he tells his wards:

In order to live properly and vigorously
Each and every person shall follow the dictates
Of his own individual consciousness of our galaxy

In other words, it is not enough for people to learn the lovely words and go through the motions of the rituals of faith. You must visualise the universe yourself and find the truth, personally, in it. Then you will come to realise that you cannot be happy until all other people in the world are happy. And if it will benefit humankind, you should, like Antares, the red giant in the constellation of the scorpion, allow your body to burn over and over again.

This is the key to Kenji Miyazawa's message to people: that you must climb the slopes of the volcano, oblivious of your own suffering, and use yourself in a scientific and social experiment; you must make your way to the sun, if necessary, to bring back its "black thorns", thereby harnessing its energy for the good of others.

Characters in his stories do just that, though clearly he was using them as vehicles for his will, just as his beloved Lotus Sutra was using – and disposing of – him in its design.

Kenji Miyazawa had the courage of his convictions, even if those convictions were occasionally exclusivist and extreme. He put his mind and body on the line, and that is something which has direct appeal to the thinking people of Japan today. In that sense, the Kenji boom itself may have heralded a new era in the reformation of individual consciousness in Japan.

But if that were Kenji Miyazawa's only legacy, then the sound of his boom would diminish over a span of distance. He provides more than just personal and concrete commitment, a means for Japanese now to feel they can make up for lost time.

He is a master stylist and a creator of the most beautiful metaphors in 20th-century Japanese poetry and prose. That, more than the example of his life, is the vehicle for his message. To paraphrase one of Kenji's poems, the lamp itself [or the body] is lost, while the light from it is preserved. The 'body' here can be read as the body of his work.

Kenji died on 21 September 1933 at his parents' home.

One of his greatest stories is 'Polano Square'. It ends with a song/prayer that ties together the various elements of Kenji's being – the poet, the believer, the teacher, and the scientist.

This story closes with the lines:

Were I to be granted my one desire
We would all be beyond the Milky Way laughing
We would burn all of our cares on a bonfire
And create a glorious new world

These lines sum up, to my mind, Kenji's ultimate desires. He wanted, more than anything, to bring light and hope to the world. The metaphor of the bonfire in the sky, burning away all our cares, is a fitting one for him and his work.

ROGER PULVERS
Tokyo

STRONG IN THE RAIN

Preface to *Spring and Ashura*

The phenomenon called I
Is a single blue illumination
Of a presupposed organic alternating current lamp
    (a composite body of each and every transparent spectre)
The single illumination
Of karma's alternating current lamp
Remains alight without fail
Flickering unceasingly, restlessly
Together with the sights of the land and all else
    (the light is preserved...the lamp itself is lost)

These poems are a mental sketch formed faithfully
Passage by passage of light and shade
Maintained and preserved to this point
Brought together in paper and mineral ink
From the directions sensed as past
For these twenty-two months
    (the totality flickers in time with me
    all sensing all that I sense)

People and galaxies and ashura and sea urchins
Will think up new ontological proofs as they see them
Consuming their cosmic dust...and breathing in salt water and air
In the end all of these make up a landscape of the heart
I assure you, however, that the scenes recorded here
Are scenes recorded solely in their natural state
And if this is nihil then it is nothing but nihil
And the totality is common in degree to all of us
    (just as everything forms what is the sum in me
    so do all parts become the sum of everything)

These words were meant to be transcribed truthfully
In the monstrous bright accumulation of time
Of the present geological era
Yet they have gone ahead and altered their construct and quality
In what amounts to a mere point of contrasted light
    (or alternatively a billion years of ashura)
Now it is possible that both the printer and I
Have been sharing a certain turn of mind

Causing us to sense these as unaltered
In all probability just as we are aware of our own sense organs
And of scenery and of people through feeling
And just as what is is but what we sense in common
So it is that documents and history...or the Earth's past
Are nothing but what we have become conscious of
Along with their diverse data
(at the root of the karmic qualifications of space-time)
For all I know in two thousand years from now
An appropriately different geology will be applied
With fitting proofs revealed one after another from the past
And everyone will surmise that some two thousand years before
The blue sky was awash with colourless peacocks
And rising scholars will excavate superb fossils
From regions glittering with iced nitrogen
In the very upper reaches of the atmosphere
Or they might just stumble
Upon the giant footsteps of translucent man
In a stratified plane of Cretaceous sandstone

The propositions that you have before you are without exception
Asserted within the confines of a four-dimensional continuum
As the nature of the mental state and time in and of themselves

Kenji Miyazawa
20 January 1924

Stop Working

Stop working
Throw down your rakes
I had all the fertiliser planned
I was responsible for the rice plants
And the paddies were flattened one after the other
Collapsing in rows
Thanks to this morning's violent thunderstorm
And half a month of cloudy sky
It is not only in the factories
That work can be demeaning
It is humbling and ignoble
To try to conceal your anxiety
By working yourself to the bone
    ...yet, ah, it's happening anew
    the school of black death seething in the west
    in the spring it was even called
    and thought of too
    as love itself...
Now, get yourself on home
Phone the weather station
Bundle your head up tight
Prepare to be soaked to the quick
Get yourself out and confront each and every person
All the many faces that are stiffened and wan
Go around encouraging them with your fire
Tell them that you will provide them compensation
Whatever it takes out of you

Love and the Fever

My soul has taken ill today
I can't even look a crow in the face
      she will burn from this moment on
      in the cold bronze sickroom
      with a translucent rose fire
Truly...yet, my little sister
I like you am too low now too
To reach willow flowers

Curse of the Lightscape of Spring

What in hell do they think they're doing
Do they have any idea?
Their black hair's trailing down
Their lips are clamped shut
That's the long and short of it, I tell you
  spring will fade, aghast, into the leaves of grass
  and all loveliness will die away!
    (it's all too pale and dark, too empty)
The light red of cheeks, the irises brown
There's no more to it than that, I'm telling you!
    (oh this bitterness this blueness this cold)

Scenery and a Music Box

The clouds are drifting rapidly, rushing
Across the bowl of dusk iced silver
Full with the bracing smell of fruit
A horse makes its way step-by-step
Between the cypresses and obsidian-like sun trees
And riding this horse is a farmer
Naturally the farmer approaching slowly
On this horse with its huge nebulous head
Finds half his body fusing
With a clump of trees and its silver-atom surroundings
He is quite amenable to this fusing
The obedient bristly Nambu horse's head droops down
Dwarfed on its way here to a black Mount Matsukura
A speck of composite dahlia
It is truly the September jewel
This lighting plan
I will present a green tomato
To the Planner of Lighting
With these soggy roads
And handrails newly coated in creosote
And two wires shining out of sham nihility
The scene seems deeply translucent
The water below thunders
A clump of down on a black swan's breast gliding along
Apples in a bracing silvered bowl of dusk
        ((ah...the moon's come out))
A radiant tapering half moon in silvered purple fabric
Polished in truly sharp autumn dust
And the angles of crystal-rimmed clouds
The handrails on the bridge are still dripping with raindrops
This whole place is simply seething with nostalgia
The water is a gently flowing body of glue
I am prepared to meet my death
In this excessively lucid landscape
At the hands of the fierce assassin who broke away
From the rough andesitic rock face of Mount Matsukura and Goken Hill
        (after all I'm the one who cut down that tree)
            (black peaks of cryptomeria pierce the sky)

The wind carries whistles half rent
    (a sorry organ of dual sensibility)
I take in the fresh green grass of ancient India
The water that strikes the cliff
Flies off on tangents like scallions
The wind blows with such thoroughness
That the surface of the half moon itself is swept clean
No wonder that my umbrella
Collapsed on the wet planks of the bridge
In a few desperate flaps
Mount Matsukura Mount Matsukura tall in the pointy dark
       bismuthic fiend sky
The electric lights are now quite hot
The wind blowing just now
Undoubtedly is the first wind of Kalpa
A motif of dawn wafting through the sky
Electric wires and a strip of terrifying chalcedonic cloud
And there a huge unexpected blue star appears
    (love's numberless redemption)
My coat flutters
With the fluttering of those terrifying bulrush-coloured clouds
    (turn on the music box, turn it on!)
The moon bifurcates without warning
A blanket of blind black haloed cloud drops over the face of light
    (be still be still, Goken Hill
    be still though your trees have been cut out of you)

Ippongino

The pines are suddenly thrown into light
The meadow bursts open
Withered grass burns under the sun inexhaustibly endlessly
Light poles are strung in a graceful line of insulators
Stretching in the imagination all the way to Bearing City
A crystal-clear sea-blue sky
And the human wish to be purified by it
Larch trees bud once again, brought back to life
A translucent lark sings its hallucinatory song
The aquamarine undulations of Mount Nanashigure
Again the rising and falling gently in the mind
A single clump of willows
Those willows along the banks of the Volga
Lie low against the malachite bowl of the heavens
Severe and unrelenting, Yakushi Rim surges up
Snow at the mouth of the crater folding in on itself
The sharpened ridge of Mount Kurakake
Hoisting nebulae into a blue sky
        (hey, Quercus
        is it true they nicknamed you
        'Backwoods Tobacco Tree')
Why have I been so graced
To spend this halfday walking at my leisure
On this grassy field and bright domed hill
I would die on the cross for these blessings
Isn't this what a lovers' tryst is like?
        (hey you, Backwoods Tobacco Tree
        you might be labelled a Futurist
        if you don't stop that bizarre dance of yours!)
As I rustle my way between the ditch reeds
With the forest and field my lovers
Modestly folded green-coloured reports
Find their way into my pockets
As I walk the darker sectors of the woods
My elbows and trousers are smothered
In imprints of crescent-moon lips

Departure to a Different Road

The earth grates at my feet
When I land alone and without destination
Between the moon's bewitchment
And this monstrous plate of snow
The void blackened by cold
Fronts hollow against my brow
    ...the musicians died with sheetlike faces
    infants came into a pale watercoloured world of mist...
A pointed blue phosphorescence
Integrates the wind thick and fast
Busily floating up and sinking down
Stitching up a blanket of snow
    ...ah, a black parade of acacia...
I have been under no illusion thus far
I have failed to live up to myself
This road that I have taken tonight
Is not the proper path
It will benefit no one
Yet I am helpless to find another way
    ...trace of the thinnest white fissure in
    a crystal sky of subdued lustre...
The snow makes it all more desolate than an ocean
With its incessant flickering

Jealous of the Dawn

The sky at dawn is about to melt
The pure fine sapphire-like planet
Sparkling, gleaming with noble light
Gathering the essence of snow and manganese spar
A short time ago the stars, strangely clear
Were casting a steady stream of blue winks
At the depths of water in that freezing sky
Its waves pitched sleepily
And the road back beyond hugged the shore
Even if the reaper does tell me,
'By the way, it's as round as they come
It's got rings and seven moons to boot
But remember that place's dead
Go and see for yourself...it's slushy!'
I'm not going to stop gazing up
At this beautiful dawn sky, grimacing
In order to love that planet all the more
Nothing will change where I set my sights
Telling me to ignore such things just puts me at a greater loss
    ...Cape Hundred and the snow-capped junipers
    and this blue sea of eternal wind
    dawning this very instant...
The stars flutter again
Like a species of bird at the point of extinction

Granddaughter of a Celebrated Buddhist Monk

A young woman made her way home
In her black work pants and straw sandal vamps
Slim, with shoulders drooping
Along an embankment of blossoming chestnut trees
She knew what there was to know
Of the ins and outs and the seasons of work
Of fertilisers and plant breeding
In all her dealings she showed transparency and tact
Her life would make a great talkie
She was standing on the levee between beds of seedlings like
        blackened teeth
Furiously flinging aside bundles of twigs
From chestnut and other trees
While discussing the causes of the year's rice blight
Who could have imagined that the big bloated monk
Who sent out his postcards again today
Then proceeded to get roaring drunk in his padded kimono
Could have given life to such a young woman
I asked a farmer the way to the house of this celebrated Buddhist
        monk
'The one livin' at the foot of the mountain,' he said
'He's famous for his gamblin' and his muddy brew'
As unsociable as they come
He was a gambler all right
His complexion and the huge wrinkles in his cheeks
Were proof enough of long nights spent in his little storehouse
Possessed by uncommon excitement
The house was kind of propped up
On a grassy slope as pretty as a park
At the base of a huge pine mountain
Girded by pitch black cryptomeria
It boasted a two-storey temple gate
And a whitewashed storehouse
Its persimmon and pear trees were radiant
But they were bone-white, eaten from the inside out
The monk had written, 'Yearly planting took place with all due care
Yet several years of sick crop resulted annually'
His penmanship was exemplary
Yet why did he take up gambling

Could it be that he merely went astray
Being too clever by half
Or could it be in his genes
Whichever, these pallid dark genes remain dormant
Inside a young woman as lovely
Grand and reliable as she
She could lead her farming village into a new era
The genes will be passed on to her descendants before awakening
Dictating neither gambling nor "muddy brew"
Where will those genes
Find their spark
Between 1950
And 2000
The west is all dim ice cloud and pale white sky
The pine forest in back, lit by the sun
Has taken on the appearance of a sea cucumber
And the faint marsh water just shines

Night

Two hours have passed now
And the blood still flows from my throat
There is not a soul walking outside
A spring night, the trees quietly breathing, sprouting
This above all is the seminary of spring
Where Bodhisattvas have given up a hundred million lives
And the Buddhas have passed into Nirvana to reside
I have resolved time and again
To die alone
Unseen tonight by anyone
Leading myself by the hand
Yet whenever the lukewarm
New blood gushes forth
Fear, indistinct, white, strikes

My Heart Now

My heart now
Is a warm sad saline lake
A pitch black lepidodendron forest stretching
Nearly five hundred miles along its shore
Must I then
Be made to sleep
Without so much as stirring
Till the reptile takes on the form of a bird?

The Winds Are Calling by the Front Door

The winds are calling by the front door
'Get yourself up and
Get out here this instant
In your sienna shirt
And that tattered old overcoat of yours'
Then another wind screams hot on its heels
'We're all here
Waiting for you to show yourself
We've got your favourite drops of sleet
Shooting across the air
So rush out, will you
And keep your promise to marry
The one among us
Who sings in a beautiful soprano voice
In the blackened leafless forest
Above the giant jagged rock in the distance'
The winds continue their screaming outside
Not letting up for a moment

Speaking with the Eyes

It's not long now
It just won't let up
It gurgles and gushes
I haven't slept all night and the blood just keeps flowing
It's blue and still out there
It looks like death...and very soon at that
And yet I feel the most magnificent breeze!
Spring is just over my shoulder
And this clear wind rushes towards me
Swelling out of that bluest of skies
The blue is the blue of a rush mat scarred by fire
A blue forming waves in a meadow of autumn flowers
In flowers like down, in young maple leaves
Dressed in your black frock coat
You may be on your way back from a medical conference
If death takes me now I can hardly complain
Seeing how diligently and cleverly you have cared for me
Could my indifference to suffering
Despite the constant flow of blood
Be a sign that the soul has half-departed the body
My sole torment is that because of this blood
I am unable to tell you this
In your eyes I am no doubt a wretched sight
But from here...after all
All I can see is that clear blue sky
And a transparent wind

Now There Is Nowhere to Turn for Money

Now there is nowhere to turn for money
The silver trail of smoke from the town
Makes its way into a glare of cirrostratus cloud

Am I Destined to Die Today

Am I destined to die today
Am I permitted to take for myself
The cumulate crown of white and black that floated in the east

We Lived Together

We lived together
A single year
She was gentle, pale
Her eyes day and night dreaming dreams far beyond me
One morning in the summer of our year
A village girl was selling flowers on a bridge on the edge of town
They were so beautiful
I bought twenty *sen* worth and took them home with me
My wife put them in an empty goldfish bowl
And displayed them in our shop
When I returned in the evening
My wife took one look at me and smiled mysteriously
I saw a spread on our table of all kinds of fruit
And white European plates
I asked her where these things came from, and she said
'I sold the flowers which you brought today for a full two yen'
        ...the stars and the blue night wind
            the reed blinds and the flame that despatches the soul...
Then that winter my wife
Without the slightest suffering
Fell ill for one day, wilted, crumbled, and passed away

Whatever Anyone Says

Whatever anyone says
I am the young wild olive tree
Dripping radiant dew
Cold droplets
Transparent rain
From my every branch

Politicians

They're just a bunch of scaremongers
Raising alarm wherever they can
And drinking their fill all the while
     fern fronds and clouds
             the world is that cold and dark
But before they know it
These fellows
Rot all on their own
Are washed away by the rains all on their own
Leaving nothing but silent blue ferns
Then some lucid geologist will come along and put this on record
As the Carboniferous Age of *man*

If I Cut Through These Woods

If I cut through these woods
The path will lead me back to that water wheel
The birds are crying dazzlingly
They may be a flock of migrating thrushes
With the southern edge of the Milky Way exploding
Radiant white throughout the night
With the fireflies streaming as never before
And, on top of that, the wind ceaselessly rocking the trees
The birds, agitated, unable to sleep
Are naturally making an awful racket
Yet
All I did was take a step into the woods
When the cries became more furious
Sharper, like a sudden downpour
What bizarre funny fellows they are!
This is a large cypress forest
With slivers of sky quivering in various ways
Breathing here and there
Between each and every pitch black branch
Messengers, so to speak, of a catalogue of light
From every possible era that is or ever was
        ...I stand in a daze, aimless
        in the birds' clamour...
The path flows dimly white to the opposite end
And Mars, muddy red, rises
From a hollow in a clump of trees
Two birds somehow slipped in unobserved
Then flew away cheerfully squeaking
Ah, the wind is blowing, carrying warmth and silver molecules
And the touch of every possible tetrahedron
When the fireflies fly in ever greater chaos
The birds' cries become denser
I hear the voice of my dead little sister
Coming from the edge of the woods
        ...even if it isn't so
        there's no need to rethink this
        for there's no difference between any of us...
The sultry fume of grass and the scent of cypress
The birds' now-deafening racket

What are they clamouring about with such fervour?
The people drawing water to their paddies
May cautiously walk the woods' borders
The stars in the southern sky may stream steadily down
Yet there is no particular danger here
It's all right to sleep your quiet sleep

Early Spring Monologue

Black hair soaked, packing rope soaked
You finally make it into the train compartment
With the daytime electric lights burning in the snowy sky
And the window glass clouded over in steam
    ...the pale light of the boulders
    the all-too-darkening patches of cypress...
You rushed, towered by crags, alone
Along that sleet-blanketed path
Carrying a bundle of charcoal nearly as tall as you
As if it were an alcove for the Guardian Deity of Children
The smoky folds in the mountains were lined up
And the dam thundered, dashing its water against the rocks
When the roots of the reeds in your bundle of charcoal
Were leaning against the walls of this goods train heading for town
They flared up red again
As if caught in an autumn drizzle
    ...the rain, translucent, is falling straight down
    the snow glides gently
    this is a bewitching spring sleet...
You stand in all modesty, drenched by the sleet
As daytime electric lights burn into the snowy sky
And over here by the dim cloudy window
You make an Egyptian veil
Out of a piece of printed red flannel
    ...the trailing skirts of enormous glacial blizzards
    sometimes encroach upon the town's gas lights
    rendering its residents placid and still...
Cold bright droplets drip
From the black cap on my head
The train runs full speed ahead
Blinking its yellow lamps
Beneath heavily cast clouds of snow

The Story of the Zashiki Bokko

This is the story of the Zashiki Bokko as we see it from here.

A bright day, and everybody had gone to the mountains to work, leaving two children in the garden to play. There wasn't a soul in the big house, so it was as quiet as the grave all around. And yet, the swishing and rustling of a broom could be heard somewhere in one of the rooms of the house.

The two children, arms firmly over each other's shoulders, went in to steal a look, but there wasn't anybody in any of the rooms, the sword box was untouched and the white cedar hedge looked bluer and bluer...there was simply not a soul in sight.

The swishing and rustling of a broom is heard.

Could it be a butcher bird calling in the distance?

Or the rush of rapids on the Kitakami River?

Is somebody winnowing beans somewhere?

The two children racked their brains, listening without making a peep, yet it did not appear to be any of these things at all. There was no doubt, though...the swish and rustle of a broom was reaching them. They snuck one more look into the rooms, but found them as deserted as before, with only the rays of the sun shining down brightly everywhere.

The Zashiki Bokko is this sort of thing.

'Ring around, round and round,' exactly ten children sang out for dear life, holding hands as they went round and round in a circle in the room. All ten children had been invited to the house for treats. They just went round and round and round and round. Then, before they knew it, the ten had become eleven. There wasn't an unfamiliar face among them, there wasn't a single identical face between them, yet any way they counted, they came up with eleven on the nose.

'The extra one is the Zashiki Bokko!' said an adult who appeared there.

But which one was the extra one? Whichever, every single child was sitting up straight as a pin, straining their eyes with all their might as if to say, 'It may be somebody else, but it ain't me!'

The Zashiki Bokko is this sort of thing.

And that's not the end of it.

The main branch of a large family always invited the children from the other branches to the Nyorai Festival at the beginning of August by the old calendar. One of those children came down with measles one year and had to stay home.

'I wanna go to the Nyorai Festival. I wanna go to the Nyorai Festival,' said the child from his bed, day in and day out.

'We'll put off the festival, so you just get better soon,' said the grandmother from the main house who had come to comfort the child. She stroked the child's head.

The child got better in September. That's when everybody was invited again. But the other children were really fed up that the festival had been put off until then and that a rabbit made out of lead had been taken away from them to console the sick child.

'He the one who's ruined everything for us!'

'Who cares if he comes. I won't play with him anyway!'

They all made a pact.

'Hey, he's here, he's here!' shouted one of the children out of the blue when they were all playing in the room.

'Okay, let's hide.'

They all rushed into the smaller next room. But wouldn't you know it, the child who had recovered from the measles, the one who had supposedly just arrived at the house, was sitting up straight in the middle of the room as frail and pale as death, looking as if he would burst into tears, holding onto a new toy bear.

'It's the Zashiki Bokko!' cried one of the children, running away.

The others followed hot on his heels.

Zashiki Bokko wept.

The Zashiki Bokko is this sort of thing.

Also, a ferryman over the waters at Romyo Temple on the Kitakami River once told me this.

'I'd drunk my fill on the night of the 17th of August by the old calendar, and hit the sack early. Then I hear this callin' from the far bank. 'Hullo, hullo!' So I get myself up and walk outta my shack and I see the moon straight up at the top of the sky. I get my boat out quick as I can, and when I get across to the other side of the river, I see a beautiful child all formal in a crested kimono and wearin' a sword. The kid stood there all by himself in white-strapped sandals. So I ask him if he wants to cross the river and he says, 'Yes, please.' He got in my boat. We reached about the middle of the river an' I was keepin' a close eye on him while pretendin' not to look. He was sittin' up straight with his hands on his knees, lookin' up at the sky. So I ask him where he's headin' and where he'd come from, and he answers in the cutest voice, 'I've been a very long time at the Sasadas', but I got bored there so I'm going somewhere else.' So I ask him why he got bored there, but all he did was smile without sayin' a word. I then asked him again where he was headed, and he said, 'I'm off to the Saitos' in Saraki.' By the time we reached the bank he wasn't in the boat anymore, and I sat myself down in the doorway of my shack. Could've been a dream, who knows? But I reckon it's true. After that the Sasadas went to the devil and the Saitos of Saraki got all their illnesses fixed up and the son there finished university, and they've really come up in the world.'

The Zashiki Bokko is this sort of thing.

Shouldering the Flowers of the Narcissus

Shouldering the flowers of the narcissus
                    white and yellow
'Mornin'!'
                    ...farmer Jacob is beaming...
'I'm just back too from selling hyacinths
Whew!
Ah, baby cabbages
I'm going to plant them along the Sen River
          but the first flood will be the end of them'
'Hey, good mornin'
Nice day'
                    the shadow of a row of pines
                    a dog...it's that yellow shaggy mutt!
                         a bird call...a bird's calling
Children on their way to school
Screaming like shrikes
Burst from the morning sun

Around the Time When the Diluvial Period Ended

Around the time when the Diluvial Period ended
And the Kitakami River settled on its present place
This area was awash with white cedars
Black alders and walnut trees
Till was carried from the mountains
During those everlasting centuries pressed with events
Deposited in places
Jumbled, scattered...
In the course of 80,000 years
With the names of the celebrated peaks
And the ancient spirits duly recorded
It now disperses into the contemporary order

Reed Cutter

The crisply cut reeds and
The purple flowers of the marsh daylily

The reed cutter stares up at the wind, his eyes
Red, inflamed

In Delirium

Invariably fair
The white and the black rising in the distance
Assume the cumulate crown

Today Without Fail I

Today without fail I
Meant to ascertain with my own two eyes
How those radiant blue gadflies
Strayed off the wind
To leap and fly inside this partition sealed by glass and rope
While I was out

Ambiguous Argument Concerning Spring Clouds

If you've been dealt a shock
By those black clouds
Blame it on mass psychology
If the tens of thousands of people similar to us
Who hoe the barleycorn fields
And cut mulberry trees
For 120 miles along this river
Transform their passion fighting the hard winter
Into a sorrowful longing
And a vague variety of hope
Then, at a loss for what to look to
They will cast their eyes to those clouds
But that's only the half of it...
That dark leaden thing
A catenary of warmed water
That is romantic love in itself
The exchange of carbon dioxide
And the sham response of spring
That is romantic love in and of itself

Sapporo City

I transformed my seething sadness
Into blue shreds of myth
In the distant sloping ashen light
And the trembling of the goods train
I scattered them with all my might
By the elms on Pioneer Memorial Square
But the little birds didn't pick at them

Smoke

The smoke from the brickwork chimneys
Forms a trail upriver
To the clouds
For two summers
I spent every afternoon after practice
Looking for long pointy fossils of walnut shell
Along the bed of white shale
That stretched, pale, from the brickworks' edge
Digging the footprints of ancient beasts
Out of thinly clouded grumbling water
Having a delightful time with my pupils
Yet now the mountains are dark on all sides
What on earth could they be burning
In the chimneys at brickworks
That had once gone so disastrously under
There is no end to the black smoke disappearing
Into the clouds that blanket the sky
The sky's most remote platinum edge
Slowly shrivels, contracting away

Spring

The sun burns, the birds cry
The oak woods sporadically
Smoke
From this day on my hands, caked
Must creak with the earth

Village Girl

The shadow of a bird crossing a field
The edge of the mountains shining bluer than blue

Pulverising the stalks of winter vegetables
With an ear to the lark and the river
She is daydreaming a conversation with someone

A Dwelling

In that crescent moon-shaped village in the south
With its blue streams
And its many hovels
They say there's no room
For a teacher-turned-seeder
    ...the light of the wind
     and the grass-seed rain...
Barefoot damp-eyed old men
Drink liquor in the afternoon sun

Shadow from the Future Zone

This blizzard is dreadful and
Again today a cave-in has come with a vengeance
    ...why are they playing that frozen whistle
    so incessantly...
A person staggers forward pale as a ghost
From the shadow and the terrifying smoke
It's no less than my own bloodcurdling shadow
Cast off from the future zone of ice

On the Train

He has sloshy raccoon hair mufflers over his ears
A black hat firmly on his head
And a vacant shadow about the eyes
    ...a plump wife and a snowbird...
He is a railway worker
Sitting resolutely by the window
Under the deepest water of these parts
    ...the wind is denser than the water
    water and ice reflect each other
    around February at Rice Marsh Field...
A spindly pine
As well as the stagnating white snowy sky
Appear on the smooth rippled window's glass surface

The Sun and Taichi

Today's sun is a small silver plate in the sky
With clouds relentlessly
Trespassing over its face
When the blizzard started shining
Taichi pulled on his red rug pants

Hill Daze

The snow sinks from the sky
Its fine slivers glistening individually
The indigo of the light pole's shadow
The glare thrown off the hills

    the hem of that farmer's raincoat
    having been cut clean off by a wind from somewhere
    is in keeping with Sanoki's woodblocks
    from the second decade of the 19th century

The meadows edge onto Siberian heavens
Seams of turquoise gleam, polished, flawless

    (the sun ceaselessly
    burns its white fire
    in a remote sky)

The snow on blades of bamboo grass
Falls in flames...falls in flames

Valley

A sediment of light
This I saw with my own eyes
Three witches
Beyond a triangular field
Their faces blotted in red pox
Plunged into some discussion
Each bent on contorting what the other says
Using glasslike steel-blue words
On a bed of dead grass

Mount Iwate

Weathered black, gouged
Into the sky's dispersed reflection
Deposited filthy white at the very bottom
Of a particle series of light

An Impression

The blue-green of the Larix is derived
From both the tree's freshness and the state of one's nerves
Just then a dark-blue gentleman in the observation car
Stood straight as a transparent pole
Tightened the X-shaped clasp on his leather belt
And ran his seemingly ailing eye
Over the mountain of light

The Swordsmen's Dance of Haratai
(mental sketch modified)

dah-dah-dah-dah-dah-sko-dah-dah
O dancers of Haratai Village
Decked in tufted cowls of black tailfeather
Brandishing your single-edge blades
Under tonight's crescent moon of strange array!
You cast the damask-rose milk of spring
Into the privations of alpen farming
You dedicate the blue-green fires of the living dawn
To the wind and the light of the plateaus
You envelope yourselves in twine and linden bark
O my friends, warriors of the atmosphere!
You intensify the white-hot lights of the sky
You gather the grief of the beech and the oak
You display signal fires in the serpentine mountains
You shake out the locks of the cypress
And blaze new nebulae
In a sky the scent of quince
    dah-dah-sko-dah-dah
You whittle your skin in humus and earth
You coarsen your sinews and bones in cold carbonic acid
You trouble yourselves each month over sunlight and wind
O paternal masters who have spent your years in piety!
On this night celebrating forest and galaxy
You sound your drums even more fiercely
Where the skyline sweeps peneplain
You reverberate the clouds clouding the palest moon
    Ho! Ho! Ho!
       long ago King Akuro of Tatta
       lived in a pitch-black cave five miles long
       crossed only by dreams and the god of darkness
       his head was chopped up fine and pickled
    And you roll Andromeda into your signal fire
       the bluster of those blue masks
       bathed in swordplay and gasping for breath
       spider's dance at the nadir of the nightwind
       puked out its writhing spindly sac
dah-dah-dah-dah-dah-sko-dah-dah

You set your blades together with yet more skill
You give off the blue tongues of immense thunder
You invite the demons of the four corners of the night
On this night of all nights when the sap shudders!
With your red robes fluttering against the ground
You deify both the wind and the hailcloud
    dah-dah-dah-dahh
The nightwind thunders the cypresses tousled
The moon a row of arrows shot through in silver light
Struck and passing on...the life of a spark
Seconds before the grating of blades dies out
    dah-dah-dah-dah-dah-sko-dah-dah
The swords' stirring a harvest lightning
The bed of the Milky Way that bears no trace
Of the rain of fire scattered into the Lion
Struck and passing on...a single life
    dah-dah-dah-dah-dah-sko-dah-dah

Pine Needles

it's that beautiful pine branch
where I gathered the sleet a little while ago
Oh...you seem to be so fired up
To press your hot cheeks against these green leaves
No one can guess our shock
At seeing you craving
These young plant needles
Your cheeks violently pierced by them
That's how eager you were to get into the woods!
And while you were in agonising pain
Sweating and burning with fever
I was happily working away in the sun
Walking about the forest with someone else on my mind
          ((ah, lovely...I feel reborn
          it's just like bein' in the woods myself))
You yearned for the woods
Like a bird like a squirrel
You must have envied me so much!
O my little sister who will travel far this day
Do you truly intend to go by yourself?
Ask me to go with you, I beg you
Cry and tell me not to stay behind
          your cheeks...yet
          such striking beauty today
          let's place this fresh pine branch
          on top of your mosquito net
          it won't take long for the drops to trickle down
          heavens
          it smells of terpene
          invigorating, can you tell?

The Morning of Last Farewell

O my little sister
Who will travel far on this day
It is sleeting outside and strangely light
    (fetch me the rainlike snow)
The sleet sloshing down
Out of pale red clouds cruel and gloomy
    (fetch me the rainlike snow)
I shot out into the midst of this black sleet
A bent bullet
To gather the rainlike snow for you to eat
In two chipped ceramic bowls
Decorated with blue watershields
    (fetch me the rainlike snow)
The sleet sloshes down, sinking
Out of sombre clouds the colour of bismuth
O Toshiko
You asked me for a bowl
Of this refreshing snow
When you were on the point of death
To brighten my life forever
Thank you my brave little sister
I too will not waver from my path
    (fetch me the rainlike snow)
You made your request to me
Amidst gasping and the intensest fever
For the last bowl of snow given off
By the world of the sky called the atmosphere the galaxy and sun
The sleet, desolate, collects
On two large fragments of granite blocks
I'll stand precariously on them
And fetch the last morsels of food
For my sweet and tender sister
Off this lustrous pine branch
Covered in transparent cold droplets
Holding the purewhite dual properties of water and snow
Now today you will part forever
With the deepblue pattern on these bowls
So familiar to us as we grew up together
(I go as I go by myself)

You are truly bidding farewell on this day
O my brave little sister
Burning up pale white and gentle
In the dark screens and mosquito net
Of your stifling sickroom
This snow is so white everywhere
No matter where you take it from
This exquisite snow has come
From such a terrifying and disarranged sky
    (when I am born again
    I will be born to suffer
    Not only on my own account)
I now will pray with all my heart
That the snow you will eat from these two bowls
Will be transformed into heaven's icecream
And be offered to you and everyone as material that will be holy
On this wish I stake my every happiness

Burning Desire's Past

I am the transmigrating puritan
Working the resplendent fields after the rain
Sniffing fresh humus mixed with the ooze
Of pale waxy sap from severed roots
The clouds swim and pitch, rushing in their directions
Each leaf of the pear tree boasts its own exquisite veins
The complete landscape of tree and sky is contained
In the lenses of droplets on the short fruit-tree branches
I am praying that those droplets will not fall
Until I have completed my circle around the tree
For after uprooting this little acacia
I will reverently bow to touch my lips to them
I must look the perfect villain
In my tattered coat and shirt with turn-down collar
Casting furtive glances
Stiffening my shoulders as if up to no good
But perhaps I will be forgiven
Nothing at all is dependable
Nothing at all can be counted on
And in a world of such phenomena
This very lack of dependability
Shows itself as this brilliant dew
It dyes the little gnarled spindle tree
Into a magnificent embroidery of colours
From red to the soft tones of moonlight
That's it, then, the acacia tree's dug out
I put down the tools, now content
I smile magnanimously as I go below a pear tree
As if meeting a waiting lover, yet
This is a burning desire
It's already turned into the watercoloured past

The Sun Sheds Slivers of Topaz

The sun sheds slivers of topaz
The clouds, rancid, are congealed in the cold
Flocks of larks rise and fall through the sky
      (why are you standing there
      you shouldn't be, you know
      an Ainu's peering in the surface of the marsh)
The south wind jolts the frozen branches
Of the one old velvet-green cryptomeria
Sending the faint white day's moth
Adrift, swaying, forlorn
Across the air's shaky shoreline
      (with the water being mercury
      and the wind carrying such balmy aromas
      this form of thinking falls well within
      the category of departed souls)
The Ainu has gone on unnoticed
The moth is now passing over the sprouting swamp cabbage along shore

The Tsugaru Strait

A shelf of black stratocumulus cloud has formed in the south
Two ancient blue-green peninsulas
Take turns to brush away the fatigue of the day
    ...two merging currents
    extracting sea fog time and again...
The waves, their hushed and glittering points
Repeated reflections in a variety of angles
Or, the weaving of stripes of silver and onion green
Or tin pest and Prussian blue
And when the water changes its costume of seven colours
Exulting in its companions
    ...a flashy and lucid wedding
    in the Oriental fashion...
The ship's smoke flows towards the south
The channel, a ghastly beautiful arsenic mirror

Before you know it, the land of Hokkaido is undulating
As rainclouds whirl their black tails
Under the northern sun

The Petals of Karma

The wind and the damp night intermingle, desolate
Blackened is the forest of willow and pine
Dark petals of karma blanket the sky
And I tremble violently from cold
For having recorded the names of gods

An Icy Joke

My dear fellow staff members: Our school has been consumed by
    a desert!
The cryptomeria forest is now a wood of Persian date palms
Our fields are gone, as are our thickets
The entire area is but an ice cloud of fine frozen sand
Mr. Shirabuchi: seeing as an Arabian genie has made his way
Straight up to about 39 degrees north latitude
Why was there no official notification from temple headquarters
The air about the place was one of jolly celebration
When we returned from class a while ago
Flowers off the silk tree and down off the goose's breast
Snowed down from the blue round of a brilliant sky
And while you were doing the binding on our term schedule
And I was building a fire
That bewitching lake of ours
Stagnated in a garish display of light
That's right...there's no doubt about it
If I were the chief abbot at your temple
It would be high time, I'd reckon, to put all your proselytisers
Atop a gigantic camel
And send them to the ends of the earth
Through opal smoke
The milky-white willow-fog of iridescence
I'd attach that massive drifting desert's virtual image to one
Or a company of soldiers or a caravan
I'd order them to stuff the pains of the world into the waterskins
Hanging off the back of hot gasping camels
And sink them, tightly sealed, in the polar sea
And then, perhaps...it would all turn into a mighty dragon
Sending violent hail storms to every corner of the globe
And at such time I, as your chief abbot
Would don a nine-stripe surplice and appear
On the Crystal Dais of temple headquarters
The top of my skull shaved bone-shiny
I'd have two attendants hold up an incense burner and a white lily
And, unruffled, with eyes raised to the sky,
I'd create a couplet of the gatha to pacify the dragon
Well, wouldn't you know it...
The journalists have finally arrived on the scene

January on the Iwate Light Railway

The snow in the rice fields glitters and sparkles
The trees along the riverbank are frozen pure white
The river back beyond slips dimly south
Lustrous and calm both its fire and ice
Hey! *Juglans Riverlander*...Walnut Tree: suspend your mirror
Hey! *Salix Riverlander*...Purple Willow: suspend your mirror
Alnus Riverlander...Black Alder: suspend your mirrormirrormirrormirror
Larix Riverlander...Japanese Larch: suspend your mirror
Light Pole Grande...Tasselled Light Pole: suspend your mirror
Juglans Riverlander...Wing Nut Tree: suspend your mirror
Morus Riverlander...Mulberry Tree: mirror
Ah-ha...this coach has finally cut across the column
The mulberry's icy flowers fall in brilliant tufts of wind

High Grade Mist

This stuff
This high grade mist is altogether too bright
The white birches have sprouted their leaves
The oat crop
The farmhouse roofs
The horses and everything under the sun
Is blindingly light
    (I am sure that you are well aware
    blue and gold in the sun
    larix the larch
    does closely resemble the fir)
There's far too much glare
Even the air hurts when I look

Cloud Signal

Ah, I'm a new man...it's such a delight
The wind is blowing and
Farm tools are shining in the sun and
The mountains are hazy...
As for the domes and pillars of volcanic rock
They're all dreaming the dreams of a timeless age
      just then a cloud signal
       was hoisted into a sky of self-denial
       in the pale spring
The mountains are hazy
Tonight the wild geese are certain
To swoop down into the four cryptomeria

A Report

The "fire" that just caused such alarm was nothing but a rainbow
For an hour on end, its cords taut across the sky

Clearing

By the time we had eventually cleared
The thicket of wild roses
The sun was blazing
The sky, a sombre pit
Me and Taichi and Chusaku
Sunk as we were into the bamboo grass
Soon dead to the world in a hollow of snores
The river drifted nine tons of needles per second
And a mass of herons flew east

Romance

A single young apple tree stands
Against a perfectly rose-coloured sky
    'Keolg Kol...hey, an owl's crying'
From the electric light on top of the hill
To the agar gelatinous illumination of the city's streets
    'Keolg Kol, is there something wrong with that?'
The boy and girl shaded in a black cloak
Sense a halo of blue light
The boy's lips smell of celery
The girl's cheeks a blossom of white clover
    'Keolg Kohl,' says the boy...
    'I shall devote myself to you for all time'

Strong in the Rain

Strong in the rain
Strong in the wind
Strong against the summer heat and snow
He is healthy and robust
Free from desire
He never loses his temper
Nor the quiet smile on his lips
He eats four *go* of unpolished rice
Miso and a few vegetables a day
He does not consider himself
In whatever occurs...his understanding
Comes from observation and experience
And he never loses sight of things
He lives in a little thatched-roof hut
In a field in the shadows of a pine tree grove
If there is a sick child in the east
He goes there to nurse the child
If there's a tired mother in the west
He goes to her and carries her sheaves
If someone is near death in the south
He goes and says, 'Don't be afraid'
If there are strife and lawsuits in the north
He demands that the people put an end to their pettiness
He weeps at the time of drought
He plods about at a loss during the cold summer
Everyone calls him Blockhead
No one sings his praises
Or takes him to heart...

That is the kind of person
I want to be

COMMENTARY
ON THE POEMS

Preface to *Spring and Ashura* (31)

In this poem, which he considers a preface to his collection of poems titled *Spring and Ashura*, Kenji sets out a proposition: that what he observes in the present is tied both to what was in the past and what will be in the future. Observation cannot be divested of sensing and feeling. Observers are a part of what they observe, and all that they see and feel is a part of them. Kenji is combining a sentient Buddhist thought with scientific method.

Our understanding of the history of the universe and everything in it is necessarily shaped and limited by our current perspective. So, according to Kenji, our view of the past will, in the future, be bound to change. Whatever is recorded by humans is recorded within the confines of a four-dimensional continuum; this is the fundamental nature of consciousness.

In this poem, Kenji suggests that in order to come to a more proper understanding of the universe and our role in it we must understand the nature of consciousness. Moreover, the continuum is based on the karma of each and every one of us and each and every object that we encounter, all intertwined in Kenji's universal fabric.

Kenji thought of his poems as – to use the phrase that he himself wrote in English – 'mental sketches modified'. In 'Preface' he speaks of his intention to transcribe these sketches truthfully, correctly. He thought of his writing not as a description of nature, but a faithful record. He often walked the fields and mountains of his native Iwate writing poems as he went, very much like a *plein air* artist.

Ashura (alternate spellings are *asura* and *shura*) is the realm of existence just below that in which humans reside. It is in this realm that we see anger and jealousy and ceaseless belligerence. Creatures, including humans, move among the six realms of existence, of which *ashura* is one. The goal is to attain enlightenment and reach paradise, thereby freeing oneself from the endless cycle. To Kenji, *ashura* was a kind of pandemonium that he was able to see in nature with his own eyes in this world.

Kenji refers to the colour blue more often than any other in his works. For him, blue signifies the other world. The wind, too, that comes from the sky carries messages from the other world, inviting you to paradise, where you will experience no more suffering.

'Preface' is Kenji's clearest statement of the way he feels about his faith, his art and his science. There is certainly no other writer in all Japan's history who was a poet, a scientist, and a devout believer all at the same time. There is no conflict between his faith and his science. The two only enhance and enrich one another.

Stop Working (33)

In this poem, which carries the date 20 August 1927, we see Kenji the agronomist. The rice crop appears to be failing, and he holds himself responsible.

The exhortation that beings with 'Now, get yourself on home' is to himself. Kenji's younger brother, Seiroku, whom I first met in the late 1960s in Hanamaki (and subsequently there and in Tokyo on a number of occasions), told me that Kenji was terrified of the rain. He had to call up all his reserves to urge himself to go out in a heavy rain like the one alluded to in 'Stop Working'. His most famous poem, appearing in this collection at the end, 'Strong in the Rain', recounts the poet's desire to be granted the strength to overcome his weaknesses and personal failings in order to come to the aid of others.

There is another element as well, though, in 'Stop Working'. It is the sensibility of one who determines to go out and 'confront each and every person', to help them in their plight. When the Kenji Miyazawa boom overtook Japan in the mid-1990s, just about the time of the centenary of his birth, it was this desire that seemed to inspire Japan's young people. They saw Kenji's active spirit, dedicated to the welfare of others and to a profound love of nature, as a guide. The message of dedicating your life to the disadvantaged, as exemplified in the life and works of Kenji Miyazawa, appealed to them in a country that had seemed, at least since the end of World War II in 1945, to be focusing its energy primarily on economic development.

A brief note on the dating of Kenji's poetry. I note the dates recorded by Kenji by saying that a poem 'carries the date...' Kenji meticulously dated his poems. But he often gave the poems dates that reflected an event – the death of his sister, the appearance of a rainbow in the sky – rather than the actual writing.

Love and the Fever (34)

When his little sister, Toshi (1898–1922), took gravely ill, Kenji was beside himself with grief. Though he was convinced that death would take her to a better place, he could not bear to see her suffer.

Kenji's poems are full of sections that are indented, parenthetical or set apart from the main body of the work. These can give, as in 'Love and the Fever', a portrait of a person or situation; they can provide scientific information about trees, rivers or other elements of nature; they can offer insight into the mind of the poet, with allusions to a Buddhist term or concept; they can also record snippets of an overheard conversation.

These lines set apart may be digressions, but they are digressions that give insight into the flow of images and ideas in Kenji's mind. This poem carries the date 20 March 1922.

Curse on the Lightscape of Spring (35)

Kenji often begins a poem with phrases spoken in a colloquial dialogue (or monologue). 'Curse of the Lightscape of Spring', which carries the date 10 April 1922, opens with 'What in hell do they think they're doing.' 'They' is the rainclouds, which he personifies here. Kenji communed with nature in a very real and intimate way.

The curse of spring, as seen in its now bright, now blackening light, carries the promise of death. Even amid the growth and light of spring there is incipient decay and darkness. Kenji is describing the *nature* of what he sees, not only the appearance.

He sees turbulence and violence in the spring, which will nevertheless give birth to life and growth. To him, it is both miraculous and terrifying, carrying the promise of death and rebirth in endless cycle.

Kenji has been compared with Walt Whitman, and the comparison is intriguing. Both poets wanted to encompass all phenomena in themselves and their work. They named as many people, objects and landscapes as they could. But Kenji is not "the poet of Japan" in the same way that Whitman is "the poet of America". There are almost no references to Japan or the Japanese people in his poems or stories, though he lived in an era of nationalism and patriotic pride.

Scenery and a Music Box (36)

This is one of Kenji's most lyrical poems, and one that beautifully illustrates his vision. 'Scenery and a Music Box' carries the date 16 September 1923.

He has gone on a walk along the Toyosawa River by Goken Hill. (The Japanese name for this hill is Gokenmori. *Mori* generally means 'forest' or 'woods', but in the dialect used in Kenji's Tohoku, the region of Japan's north in which Hanamaki is located, it means 'hill'.)

Kenji has taken this walk to cut down trees in the early evening. It is rainy and windy, then the sky clears, and the wind becomes gentler. Kenji sees in this calmer wind a signal of *kalpa*. 'Kalpa' is a term in Buddhism that signifies an extremely long period of time. To Kenji, a Nichiren Buddhist, it represents not only time itself, but the formation and disintegration of the world. 'An eternity' might be another way of putting it. Kenji is taking his walk at dusk. But he sees in this fresh breeze a motif of dawn (he uses the English word 'motif' here, in the 11th line from the end).

Nambu is the district near the town of Morioka (known traditionally for its ironworks). A Nambu horse has a relatively large head and a robust constitution.

The sounds of the 'music box' of the poem are actually sounds made by the electric wires as they shake in the wind. Because the wind produces this music, these sounds may be interpreted as telling us of the world beyond.

The 'speck of composite dahlia' is a metaphor for the electric light that Kenji sees along the road, and which he equates with 'the September jewel', the sapphire.

At the end of the poem, Kenji implores nature, in the form of the hill, to be still. He has taken something – the trees he cut down – from nature, and fully expects nature to respond by taking something from him, even his life. This very Buddhist theme appears in other places in Kenji's work. For instance, the bear hunter in the story 'The Bears of Mount Nametoko' is destined to be dealt with by the bears he has tracked all his life.

The double parentheses appear in the original.

Ippongino (38)

Kenji is walking on the Ippongino Plain in the village of Takizawa in this poem that carries the date 28 October 1923. Though it is autumn ('the withered grass burns'), the larch trees seem to be putting out new leaves and a lark sings...or is this just an hallucination?

Mount Nanashigure lies some 20 kilometres to the north. Yakushi Rim is the highest cliff on the volcanic Mount Iwate, the prefecture's highest mountain. Kurakake is a part of Mount Iwate.

As the poet walks, his imagination gets away from him, and he sees willows along the banks of the Volga. The Bearing City that he refers to also exists only in Kenji's imagination.

As for the Backwoods Tobacco Tree, there had been a custom, among farmers of the region, of smoking the leaves of the local oak when they couldn't get their hands on anything better.

Kenji Miyazawa is perhaps the only modern Japanese writer in whose works sex plays no part and romance very little. This comes from his very ascetic religious beliefs. But we see in his poetry, and in this poem, an erotic link with nature. He walks the meadow, the hill and the woods. He takes it all in. He can't get enough of it. He is ready to die for the blessing of having a half day by himself in the lap of nature. The folded leaves find their way into his pockets; and, in the 'darker sector of the woods', where he is truly alone with nature and unseen, leaves shaped like crescent moons – probably of the tickseed plant that grows there – cling to his arms and his clothing like kisses.

Departure to a Different Road (39)

Between the 5th and 9th of January 1925, Kenji travelled along the Sanriku Coast, where the Tohoku region meets the Pacific Ocean. (He dated this poem 5 January 1925.) This rugged district has almost no railway line even now. On this particular trip Kenji went, among other places, to Kamaishi, Miyako and Kuji. The winter climate there is severe. This is not the gentle, exquisite, and delicate Japan of Kyoto and Nara that has largely come to represent the core of the Japanese aesthetic around the world.

Kenji constantly measures himself against his ideals, feeling that he has failed in what he sees as his obligations to the farmers of Iwate. This confrontation with the landscape and moonlit sky brought home to him his shortcomings all the more ('I have failed to live up to myself').

Kenji often writes of the 'correct' or 'proper' path. This refers to his commitment to Nichiren Buddhism. Nichiren was a 13th-century Buddhist priest who put the Lotus Sutra at the centre of his faith, and preached that every individual can attain enlightenment.

In 'Departure to a Different Road', the poet writes of feeling desolate and lost, 'alone and without destination'. This poem is a perfect example of the way that Kenji's inner world and the things he observes outside it are fused.

The 'white fissure' that he manages to catch sight of in the sky is probably the Milky Way. To him, the blue phosphorescence is no doubt a sign from the other world, and the Milky Way, a road to reach it.

Jealous of the Dawn (40)

This poem was written on the same trip as 'Departure to a Different Road'. It describes what Kenji saw before dawn on 6 January 1925 and carries that date.

On that night, in the Sanriku district, Saturn, Venus and Mercury were visible in the predawn sky. In Kenji's works, 'the sapphire planet' is Saturn, and there is no doubt here that Kenji and 'the reaper' are discussing that planet. The sky is about to 'melt' the planets and stars. In other words, their light will fade in the light of the rising sun.

Once again Kenji combines the lyrical with the colloquial. The language of the reaper in the quotation is that of a local farmer.

The deep water and the waves that Kenji describes are not in the ocean, but rather in the sky. This same imagery appears in a later poem in this collection titled 'On the Train' (see page 70).

Again, too, we see the word 'love' used in connection with something in nature. Kenji's view of nature is not that of an observer on the verandah of a temple garden describing subtle beauty in an understated fashion. He threw himself into nature body and soul. There are a number of words for 'love' in Japanese, and the one Kenji uses here, *koi*, indicates passionate love. *Koisuru* is a verb meaning 'to be in love' or 'to make love'. He is jealous of the dawn because it has the power to melt his lover.

Granddaughter of a Celebrated Buddhist Monk (41)

'Granddaughter of a Celebrated Buddhist Monk' is, like 'We Lived Together' (see page 49), a poem that has a narrative. The heroine is the hard-working, upright young woman who 'could lead her farming village into a new era'. She is educated in agronomy. She is the new type of farmer that Kenji envisaged for his beloved Iwate.

But her grandfather is a corrupt monk, a gambler and a drinker. In his short story 'Snow Crossing', Kenji makes it clear that he considers drinking and indolence to be unacceptable vices. Kenji Miyazawa is a moralist, and he desires to reform the old customs that stand in the way of progress.

In this poem, which is undated, he refers to 'genes'. He knows there are genetic predispositions towards certain behaviour. But here he puts these predispositions into the context of karma. The trees in front of the old monk's house may be beautiful, but they are eaten out from the inside. It is this rottenness inside that will surely surface again in people born into this family. The monk's seed itself is rotten.

As a devout follower of Nichiren, Kenji felt disdain for Buddhists who adhered to other sects. This disdain is expressed clearly here.

Nature, in the form here of an icy pale sky, pine trees in the sun, and the surface of the marsh, looks upon this cycle in human life year after year.

Night (43)

Kenji often describes death in his poetry and stories. He doesn't prettify conditions or spare the details. Here he is describing his own suffering from tuberculosis that causes him to bleed through his mouth. This poem carries the date 28 April 1929, more than four years before he actually died.

He sees this spring night, with its trees sprouting new leaves, as a seminary for Buddhist monks, as a place where humans have sacrificed their lives for the welfare of others and attained Buddhahood. But despite his faith in what lies ahead for him, he is just a human being after all, full of pain and fear. Though he is alone, he does not express self-pity here. He is ready, on this night, for his death.

My Heart Now (44)

This poem is also written in illness, at about the same time as 'Night'. Kenji chose here the metaphor of a saline lake to describe his heart.

The lepidodendron is a tree that was prolific during the Carboniferous Period, 360 to 286 million years ago. It was a gigantic tree that could grow to be over thirty metres in height. These trees formed ancient coal forests, and Kenji would definitely have thought of this in selecting the tree for the poem. Coal can be used for the good of humankind, in providing energy for modernisation of the countryside. There is a specimen of a lepidodendron fossil in the Museum of Natural History at Tohoku University. This fossil is pitch-black, and it is likely that Kenji saw it.

One more thing about this tree that has associations with Kenji. It was very tall, with all its branches at the top. It looked a little like an electric light pole. Kenji liked to draw light poles with a head on them, their crossbeams representing arms. He may have been drawn to this tree for more reasons than one.

In this poem, Kenji is wondering what will happen after he dies, what form the world will have taken when he awakens, millennia from now.

The Winds Are Calling by the Front Door (45)

In his novel *Night on the Milky Way Train*, passengers on that celestial railway pass by a forest and hear beautiful music coming from it. In this poem, voices come to Kenji on the wind. These voices are insistent and demanding. And now they are not in the distance as seen from a railway carriage window, but right at his front door, not letting up for a moment.

Kenji wrote this poem in the late 1920s, after falling ill from fatigue and overwork. Like the two preceding poems and the one that follows this, it is from his cycle of poems titled 'While Convalescing'.

Speaking with the Eyes (46)

This poem depicts an encounter between a man who believes he is dying and his physician. The blood keeps flowing from Kenji's mouth, and he assumes that he is close to death. The vision before his eyes is of a transparent wind in a clear blue sky: the entrance to paradise.

The dying man has no complaints. Tuberculosis was the AIDS of his era. Rest and a diet rich in protein and nutrition might have prolonged his life. But Kenji was a vegetarian and worked indefatigably for his people. His own health was just one concern, and one seemingly not as important to him as the wellbeing of others.

His 'sole torment' is that, because of the blood, he is unable to speak, except with his eyes. He also has the ability to see himself through the eyes of his doctor ('In your eyes I am no doubt a wretched sight'); this meaning is also contained in 'speaking with the eyes'.

In the original Japanese, the word *chi* ('blood') appears three times. Kenji's physical suffering is expressed more clearly in this poem than in any other. Yet he is still able to see the beauty of nature in the sky, the wind, the flowers and the young maple leaves.

Now There Is Nowhere to Turn for Money (47)

The trail of smoke winding upward from a factory chimney is an image that appears several times in his poetry. Silver is, of course, associated with money. But the character *gin* ('silver') is also one of the two characters used to write *ginga* ('the Milky Way').

In this poem, which carries the date 30 June 1927, we sense the economic fate of provincial towns in northern Japan. Throughout most of the 20th century, Iwate was often referred to as 'the Japanese Tibet', implying poverty and a lack of development. In one of his stories, Kenji creates a character who thinks of climbing up to the sun to fetch its "black thorns". Kenji wanted to do whatever he could to harness the energy that was needed to bring his home district into the 20th century.

That desire makes this little poem all the more poignant.

Am I Destined to Die Today (48)

This poem carries the date 13 June 1927, more than six years before Kenji died.

The crown that he refers to is a crown of cloud. Kenji knows that if he dies, his soul will transmigrate through the heavens. The crown of cloud is a metaphor for his passing into another state of existence. This is a source of both terror and joy, but he accepts his fate.

We Lived Together (49)

'We Lived Together', which carries a date in 1927 only 12 days before the previous poem was written, stands out in Kenji's poetry as a rare romantic portrayal of a marriage. As in many of his poems the women are strong and resourceful. Kenji recognised that women in the Japanese countryside work every bit as hard as men, sometimes harder.

But for Kenji, who never experienced a romantic or sexual relationship, this single year of married bliss has a fairytale quality. Most of his poems are firsthand descriptions of nature, either snapshots like 'Mount Iwate' in this collection (see page 74), or rambling narratives like his longest poem, 'Koiwai Farm' (not included in this volume). He also describes local events, such as the swordsmen's dance of Haratai Village (see page 76), writes parables of nature and morality ('Ambiguous Argument Concerning Spring Clouds', page 63), or goes deep within to depict aspects of his own psyche ('Whatever Anyone Says', page 50, and 'In Delirium', page 61).

As early as the third line, we get an inkling that the wife is going to die. He describes her as pale, using the word *aojiroi*. This can also be translated 'pallid' or 'wan'. Literally the characters mean 'blue-white', however, and blue is always, for Kenji, a colour that suggests the world beyond. A similar suggestion is made in the fourth line. This dream of hers that he cannot understand is certainly a premonition of her death. (A similar guarded reference is made in his novel *Night on the Milky Way Train*.) The wife smiling mysteriously that evening only reinforces the impression that she expects her fate. After all, the fishbowl is empty, so the fish must have died as well.

The European plates on the table signify that this evening is special. Perhaps this is intended to celebrate the sale of the flowers. Two yen was, at the time, a considerable sum of money, representing a price that is ten times the purchase price. But the two lines set apart give an indication of why this night might be special. These lines contain the stars, the wind, blueness, the spirit (or soul) and fire: in other words, all the elements that are necessary to transport a person from the human realm to a realm that is higher. Up to this point, this story has been rather mundane, with pottery, fruit, and flowers and a down-to-earth theme. But these two lines lift it to the plane that Kenji has in mind here.

When the wife dies, she dies withering and crumbling, like a flower. The word that denotes withering is *shioreru*. This can be translated as 'wither', 'wilt', 'fade' or 'droop'. There is even a meaning of languishing in an illness or in sadness. *Shioreru* can also connote a loss of energy and spirit: to be down in the dumps, glum, crestfallen or dejected. But here the image is of a flower wilting.

Kenji tells us that the wife did not suffer at all. She may have been in pain, but she did not suffer, because she knew that she was destined to go to a better place, where there was nothing but a transparent wind. His description of her death at the end is written in a matter-of-fact manner in Japanese, almost like a dry report in a document. This was her fate, and that's all there is to it. Sad, yes, but inevitable.

Whatever Anyone Says (50)

Kenji knew that he was out of step with his times and was aware that people thought him highly eccentric. In his best-known poem, 'Strong in the Rain', the last one in this volume, he aspires to be a man others call 'a blockhead'.

In 'Whatever Anyone Says', which carries the date 3 May 1927, he imagines himself a tree in the rain. He uses the word *sukitotta* ('transparent'), which is a key word that he often uses to indicate the world beyond. He ends the poem with a formal form of the verb 'to be', *de aru*. He uses this formal language in a number of poems, and it gives them a nuance that sounds almost as if he were delivering this statement to a committee. To me, this is the scientist Kenji Miyazawa at work. He is examining and describing reality, whatever anyone may say about science or about him.

Politicians (51)

Though some people in Japan think of him as a kind of hermit-bard, Kenji Miyazawa was no recluse. He was gregarious and aspired to sociability, though he was motivated by an extreme didacticism and religious fervour. He was intensely concerned with the events around him.

The era of his adulthood – that of Taisho (1912–26) and early Showa Japan (the Showa Era represents the reign of Emperor Hirohito, 1926 to 1989) – was characterised by political and cultural polemics, the emergence of so-called proletarian literature and ever-increasing Japanese nationalism.

As was mentioned in the Introduction, as an eldest son, Kenji was exempt from conscription. But it remains an open question whether he would have supported, as did the vast majority of Japanese intellectuals, the Japanese imperial cause in Asia. He threw himself into proselytising work in Tokyo on behalf of the Kokuchukai, a fascist-leaning patriotic Buddhist organisation.

This portrait of politicians, dated on the same day as the previous poem, is cutting. He refers to politicians collectively as *yatsura*, a disrespectful term for a bunch of men who are, in this case, up to no good. His approach to counter these rotters is not to enter into a polemic against them. He knows that in time they will die away 'all by themselves'. Nature will take its course with regard to them.

Kenji's geological time span is underscored by the ferns in the poem. The fern is an ancient plant, predating the beginning of the Mesozoic era. That makes it more than 350 million years old, older than the dinosaurs and 200 million years older than flowering plants.

Kenji often uses the word *tomei*, meaning 'transparent', 'translucent' or 'crystal clear' (*tomei* is basically the same word as *suki-toru*, in a different form). But when *tomei* is used to modify a word like 'scholar', it comes to mean 'earnest'. I have tried to express this play on words with the adjective 'lucid'.

If I Cut Through These Woods (52)

Some of Kenji's best poems were produced in response to the death of his little sister, Toshi. Perhaps the most famous of those is 'The Morning of Last Farewell' (see page 79).

He cannot forget her, and imagines himself communicating with her through nature. 'The southern edge of the Milky Way' brings to mind the train that travelled along it from north to south, transporting people to their final resting-places among the stars.

There is a sense of real agitation, though, in this poem. The fireflies are 'streaming as never before'. For this 'streaming' he uses the verb *nagareru*, which describes how a river flows. The wind is ceaselessly (*hikkirinashi ni*) rocking the trees, and the birds are unable to sleep. His presence only augments the racket.

But perhaps the most amazing thing about Kenji's poetry is, to my mind, his descriptions of light. I can think of no other Japanese poet who describes light in such an exquisite and varied way. Here is a passage from *Night on the Milky Way Train*. The train that Giovanni is on has just arrived at Milky Way Station.

> And before his eyes there was a flash flood of intensely bright light, as if billions and billions of phosphorescent cuttlefish had fossilised at their most radiant instant and been plunged into the sky, or as if someone had discovered a hidden cache of precious jewels that the Diamond Company had been hoarding to bolt the price sky-high, turning the whole treasure topsy-turvy and lavishing them throughout the heavens. Giovanni found himself rubbing his eyes over and over, blinded by the sudden dazzle.

In 'If I Cut Through These Woods', the starlight filters down through the trees of the forest, carrying 'a catalogue of light from every possible era that is or ever was'. Kenji is commenting on the fact that the light from stars farther away comes from a time in the more distant past. The entire sky to him is this 'catalogue of light'.

This poem carries the date 5 July 1924. Mars' closest approach to Earth occurred in August of that year, and Kenji would have had a good view of the red planet in the late-night summer sky. July is also the time of year when rice farmers irrigate their paddies.

The last line of the poem is addressed to his sister.

Perhaps it is not for a translator to comment critically on the poems that he has translated; but I cannot resist the temptation to say that 'If I Cut Through These Woods' is a stunning poem that beautifully illustrates Kenji's deepest concerns.

Early Spring Monologue (54)

Kenji paints many portraits of farming and working people in his poems. Here he encounters a woman carrying a huge bundle of charcoal on her back. The woman has rushed along a mountain path in a horrendous storm to catch her train. No doubt she is headed into town, to sell her charcoal.

The woman in 'Early Spring Monologue' is carrying her bundle as if it were 'an alcove for the Guardian Deity of children' (*jizo bosatsu*). Statues of Jizo can be seen throughout Japan, many of them erected by the sides of roads. This lends an image of holiness and compassion to the woman's work.

Once again, as in 'Scenery and a Music Box', we see in this poem, which carries the date 30 March 1924, a picture of the violent climate characteristic of the Tohoku region. The sky is laden with snow clouds, and the poor woman, anxious to make her train, is 'drenched by the sleet'. But Kenji calls this spring sleet 'bewitching'. The character that he uses here is associated with the supernatural, and the word has those nuances, with 'marvellous', 'uncanny' and 'mysterious' in it for good measure. Nature has the uncanny power to make people 'still'.

As for Kenji, drops of rain fall from his cap (he uses the then fashionable word *shappo*, borrowed from the French *chapeau*).

Finally, the title. This is not only meant to be a monologue by the poet; it is a monologue spoken by spring itself. Kenji is not describing this scene, but recording it as it is narrated by the phenomena of nature before his eyes.

The Story of the Zashiki Bokko (55)

This prose poem is a wonderful illustration of Kenji's view of children, illness, and fate. The mystery-child is often evoked in his stories as a messenger or seer. *Zashiki* means 'room', and *bokko* here means 'child'. So a Zashiki Bokko is simply a little boy who appears in a room...is this one an apparition? Sometimes it appears as sound, or in the form of a sick child. Did the poor little boy here, I wonder, die of measles and appear to the children and the ferryman after death, despite the fact that Kenji says he recovered? The ferryman claims that he did carry the boy in his boat, but the boy vanished from sight. (The ferryman admits that he had been drinking.)

Perhaps a clue to these questions resides in the reference to the Nyorai Festival. A *nyorai* is an individual who has attained Buddhahood. The boy may be a symbol of enlightenment.

Shouldering the Flowers of the Narcissus (58)

Kenji's poems are full of references to flowers, including narcissus and hyacinths as in this poem, as well as lotus flowers and bellflowers, to name just a few. Here flowers are being sold by people in the village. He even gives one of the villagers a foreign name, Jacob, which may be a Biblical reference. Kenji's characters often have non-Japanese names.

The conversation is very colloquial, though it is not written in his native dialect. In fact, while colloquial, the tone is also rather polite. There is, to my mind, a suggestion of a rural idyll in this poem. The reference to flooding, however, reminds us that catastrophe, in the form of flooding or drought, is always around the corner for these farmers.

A bird is calling, and the pine grove casts a shadow. But then it might not be a bird at all, but rather the happy children on their way to school, 'bursting from the morning sun'.

'Shouldering the Flowers of the Narcissus' carries the date 21 April 1927.

Around the Time when the Diluvial Period Ended (59)

In Kenji's day it was thought that the glacial era ended some 80,000 years ago, though today it is known to have ended approximately 10,000 years ago.

At the end of that period, the Kitakami River, which runs through Hanamaki, was formed in more or less its present state. This is the river that Kenji knew so well, explored and loved. He collected all sorts of rocks from the area as a child and was given the nickname 'Little Rocky Kenji'. He also picked up petrified walnut shells that presumably had fallen off trees 'during those everlasting centuries'. Kenji's brother, Seiroku, gave me just such a shell in 1970, telling me that Kenji had picked it up on the bank of the Kitakami River.

In his poetry Kenji is not content with capturing a sublime moment in time, as are many Japanese poets. When he looks at nature, he cannot help but see its distant past, encompassing that vision into the poem's image. Humans who lived by the Kitakami River gave names to mountains and to their gods. The 'contemporary order' as we know it is the result of the chaos of dispersion ('jumbled, scattered') and the mind of the human beings who recorded what they saw. Kenji sees himself as a chronicler of natural events.

'Around the Time When the Diluvial Period Ended' carries the date 21 March 1927.

Reed Cutter (60)

This is a portrait of a farmer working hard at cutting reeds. But he takes a moment to look up at the wind (*sawayaka*, 'crisp', is a word often associated with wind). He may be keeping an eye on the weather, hoping to finish his job before a storm sets in. But to Kenji the wind can be a portent: it is the wind that comes from the world beyond to snuff out the flame of the candle of life (this is the way that Kenji's brother, Seiroku, described it to me).

The marsh daylily referred to here is called *mizugiboshi* in Japanese. It is rarely seen in Kenji's Tohoku district, and is more common in western Japan. It has elongated pointed oval leaves and, in summer, funnel-shaped flowers.

This poem carries the date 7 July 1927.

In Delirium (61)

This poem, which carries the date 13 June 1927, presents the same image, of a crown of cloud, as 'Am I Destined to Die Today' (see page 48). Here, however, Kenji uses the imperative. In his delirium, he is ordering himself to be unafraid of death. The clouds are black (ominous) and white (deathlike).

Today Without Fail I (62)

Once again Kenji turns his scientist's eye to a simple occurrence. It is this eye that distinguishes him from virtually all other Japanese poets.

Kenji returned home to find 'those gadflies' (he has seen them before) inside what he thought to be a sealed container. He is determined to get to the bottom of this event, and the final formal use of the verb *de aru* ('to be') gives this one-sentence poem a kind of official seriousness.

The gadflies that have 'strayed off the wind' are blue and radiant. This gives them a symbolic presence as messengers from beyond.

'Today Without Fail I' carries the date 12 May 1927.

Ambiguous Argument Concerning Spring Clouds (63)

This may be one of Kenji's most difficult poems to fathom. It describes a scene in spring, when he is farming the land with his fellow farmers (the poem carries the date 5 April 1927) and black clouds appear in the sky. He argues that farmers all along the river, just like them, will also be casting their eyes to those clouds. They have fought off the hard winter with passion and now harbour both sadness and hope.

They see in the sky 'that dark leaden thing, a catenary of warmed water'. What a remarkable metaphor for clouds! A catenary, according to *The Shorter Oxford English Dictionary*, is a 'curve formed by a chain or rope of uniform density hanging freely from two fixed points not in the same vertical line'. (The Dutch scientist Christiaan Huygens was the first to use this term, in a letter to

Leibniz in 1690.) The scene, then, that Kenji is depicting is of low, drooping black clouds. Naturally this is very worrying to the farmers.

But he reassures them. He urges them to look at the clouds and understand that they represent phenomena indicating real love. Again, Kenji is finding romance (the word he uses for 'love', *renai*, is the term for tender, passionate, romantic love) in nature. This is what he is so desperate for others to see along with him.

Sapporo City (64)

Sapporo is the largest city in Hokkaido, the island to the north of the main island of Honshu. This poem carries the date 28 March 1927. Kenji visited Hokkaido a number of times.

Trips north are generally associated in his poetry with the death of his little sister (see 'The Morning of Last Farewell', page 79). Kenji travelled as far north as Sakhalin out of loneliness, perhaps in search of a way to communicate with Toshi.

In this poem he is alone. The train is 'trembling'. In the distance is an 'ashen light'. Ash, of course, symbolises death. The colour blue here reinforces that symbolism.

When Kenji arrives in the city, he scatters his sad feelings like seeds. The birds might eat them and spread them far and wide. But they don't.

Here Kenji recognises his isolation from society. There is also a hidden reference to another poet from Iwate, one whom he admired immensely, Takuboku Ishikawa. The character Kenji uses for 'to pick at' is one of the characters used to write Takuboku's name. I don't think this a coincidence.

Takuboku, too, had gone to Hokkaido alone, but he had found solace there in the form of female company, something that Kenji would never have dreamt of seeking.

Smoke (65)

Kenji delighted in these walks on the bank of the Kitakami River that flows through his hometown of Hanamaki. He would don the full gear from straw hat to gaiters and carry a clinometer for measuring angles, a jeweller's eyeglass and a little hammer.

The pointy walnut shells that are found in the area are from the *batagurumi*, a type of walnut that grew along the river in the Tertiary Period and is now extinct. That section of the river, with its white rock, reminded Kenji of Dover (where, needless to say, he had never been). He named it 'the English Coast', which it is called to this day. The 'footprints of ancient beasts' are hollows in the rock apparently left in the Tertiary Period by mammoths.

In 'Poem of the English Coast' (not included in this collection) he writes, 'This is certainly the foreshore of ashura.' In other words, he saw the waterline on the bank as the border to another realm of existence, the realm of pandemonium. This accounts for the use of 'pale' in the poem and for the ominous turn towards the end, when the mountains suddenly go dark on all sides.

The brickworks went bankrupt a long time ago, and yet there is thick black smoke, another sign of the transience of life, curling up towards the sky. What is the meaning of this smoke? Could it be a link between people's toil, that is, their physical state on this earth, and the state of the soul once it has begun its trip into the sky and beyond?

'Smoke' carries the date 9 October 1926. Despite the poem's rather gloomy portent, Kenji here is looking back fondly at excursions with his pupils.

Spring (66)

Kenji has decided to become a full-time farmer. He moves into a house owned by the Miyazawa family on the outskirts of Hanamaki. (If you visit this house you may see a sign, written in a hand to resemble Kenji's that reads: 'I am in the field below.') It was here that he cooked for himself, worked in the fields from early in the morning and indulged in his various hobbies at night, such as studying languages and playing his cello. One imagines a very lonely life for Kenji in this period.

The birds' cries and the smoke give this little poem an atmosphere of otherworldliness typical of Kenji.

The mimetic word that Kenji uses for creaking hands is *gichigichi*. But he adds the verb *naru*, or 'cry out', to *gichigichi*, almost giving the impression that his hands are like the birds.

Kenji's people were not farmers, and for him to make this transition was in no way easy. I cannot help but feel that the exertion and hard work took a toll on his health and eventually hastened his demise.

'Spring' carries the date 2 May 1926.

Village Girl (67)

This is a pastoral scene centred around a farm girl. As she works, there is something on her mind, and she is daydreaming.

The shadow of the bird and the blue-shining edge of the mountain are, once again, often-expressed Kenji images that suggest communication between the person in the poem and the natural and supernatural worlds.

Kenji dated this poem 2 May 1926, as he also did 'Spring'.

A Dwelling (68)

There exists a shorter poem that is similar to this one, with the same title. It is one of a handful of poems of Kenji's that he himself translated into Esperanto. In that poem, the line 'the wind's light' appears as 'a silver monad'.

The villages of rural Japan were often poor, with tenant farming the norm. The one in this poem has no time for a 'teacher-turned-seeder', presumably Kenji himself. The term for 'seeder' used here is *taneya*. The *ya* at the end shows a certain disdain for the person bringing the seeds. Kenji often found himself rebuffed by the very farmers to whom he was trying to introduce modern farming methods.

The old men drinking in the midday sun represent the bad old ways of the village. In his story 'Snow Crossing', Kenji portrays some people in the village as drunk and immoral. Needless to say, he himself did not touch liquor for reasons of faith.

Kenji seemed to have the ability to see himself as others did, as in the case of this teacher-turned-seeder. He realised how far removed he was from his times, and this was, I believe, a great cause of his sadness. He burned with the desire to show people his way.

'Dwelling' carries the date 10 September 1925.

Shadow from the Future Zone (69)

There are two future zones in Kenji's poetry, and they reflect his ambiguity towards the future itself. On the one hand, he believed that the future for all who tread 'the proper path' (as dictated by his form of Buddhism) was bright. He expresses this in a poem written for his pupils in which he says:

Don't you feel the transparent pure wind
Blowing towards you from your future zone

In later lines he goes on to label this wind 'a southerly' (the Milky Way train runs from north to south). These lines were found after Kenji's death by his brother Seiroku in the form of notes written in red ink. It is thought that the date of their composition was sometime in 1927.

But in 'Shadow from the Future Zone', which carries the date

15 February 1925, the image is even darker, with its 'frozen whistle' coming from the beyond.

'A person staggering forward pale as a ghost' has all of the imagery of the so-called *jigoku-e*, the 'pictures of Hell' from the Kamakura Period (1185–1333). In this case, however, it is *ashura* – another realm of existence entirely – and not hell, from which the shadow is cast. The mimetic word *yoroyoro* is used here. It suggests faltering, tottering, or staggering, all types of walking that someone either old or infirm would display. The adjective for shadow that I have rendered as 'bloodcurdling' is *senritsu subeki*. *Senritsu subeki* suggests the kind of terror that makes the flesh creep, a very strong epithet even for Kenji.

Kenji is known in his poems and stories for not making death look pleasant or easy. Despite the fact that Kenji is certain that he will go to a better place, the coldness of it all continues to horrify him.

On the Train (70)

Here is another realistic portrait of an ordinary worker, in this case not a farm worker, but a railway track maintenance man (Kenji identifies the man as such in another shorter but similar poem). But the setting, while mundane, is far from realistic. The worker sits by the window, apparently unperturbed that the scene seen through the rippled glass is underwater.

This poem carries the date 5 February 1925. The man at the window is staring into the future, a place where the wind is denser than water.

The word for 'vacant' is *utsuro*, and its sound connects with the last word of the poem in the original, *utsusu*, which literally means 'reflects'. Kenji may be the Japanese poet of the 20th century who is most closely attuned to the sound of words taken together. That is why his poems lend themselves so well to recitation.

There are numerous references in the poem to water, including 'sloshy', 'snow', 'ice', 'marsh', 'snowy' and 'rippled'. Kenji often exchanges air for water, as he does life for what comes after.

The Sun and Taichi (71)

This poem carries the date 9 January 1922.

Taichi has evidently been waiting for the snowstorm to clear before going out to work in the fields.

The name Taichi appears again in Kenji's work (see 'Clearing', page 90). When the French novel *Rémi sans famille* was translated into Japanese and became a bestseller (under the title *Ienakiko Remi*, or Remi the Homeless Child), the translator changed the name of one of the characters to Taichi. This sort of adaptation was not all that uncommon in the translations of stories and plays in the Japan of the Meiji Era. Kenji was known to have loved this book and probably took the name Taichi from it. The name Chusaku that appears in 'Clearing' seems to have come from Kenji's imagination.

Hill Daze (72)

'Hill Daze' carries the date 12 January 1922. It depicts a midwinter scene in the north.

The light, or telephone, pole commonly appears in Kenji's poetry and stories. It is obviously a symbol of modernisation and communication in a part of Japan that was economically backward and remote. Kenji went so far as to personify these poles, sketching them with a head and arms. (Kenji left behind many drawings and paintings.) Perhaps he saw himself as just such a light pole.

The scale of things described in his poems can jump suddenly from the vast and abstract to the carefully observed detail of everyday life. (This is a feature seen in traditional haiku as well.) All of a sudden, amid the glare of the snow sinking from the sky, we are drawn to the hem of a farmer's raincoat. Sanoki was a publisher of woodblock prints who published, among others, works of Hiroshige and Kunisada. Kenji was enamoured of woodblock print art and had a collection of his own. It is even said that he owned *shunga*, or erotic prints, though this is only rumour. Some years ago, before a trip to Hanamaki on which I was set to meet Kenji's brother, Seiroku, I was approached by a leading publisher, who was also a friend of mine, with a proposition. If I could somehow get my hands on Kenji's erotic woodblocks, they would publish them. 'We'd have a guaranteed print run of a million copies,' said my publisher friend. Up in Hanamaki I had a lovely 90-minute meeting with Seiroku, with us reciting Kenji's poetry to each other. But, I must admit, I didn't have the nerve to bring up the topic of the woodblocks. Call it propriety, or decorum, but I just didn't feel right about it, despite the prospect of a print run of a million copies looming large in my mind. So, the mystery of Kenji's erotic prints remains to be solved – and the bestseller, published – by some other Kenji admirer.

Siberia and Russia in general, places to which Kenji never journeyed, figure from time to time in his poems. Here Siberia is a place where the sky ends, a metaphor of the beyond...a perfect setting for snow that falls like fire.

Valley (73)

This poem carries the date 20 April 1922. It is early spring. Kenji often sees black portents in the spring. After all, his major collection of poems is called *Spring and Ashura*.

This poem strikes me as a little portrait of the valley of hell. The word for 'witch' is *yojo*, which can also mean 'temptress' or 'vampire'.

The language of the original is slightly formal, ending with *desu*.

Mount Iwate (74)

Mount Iwate stands over the district of Kenji's homeland much as Mount Fuji does over the Kanto Plain. Seen from the Koiwai Farm, about which Kenji wrote his longest poem, it is particularly beautiful.

But to Kenji, Mount Iwate was no picture postcard. During his seven years at Morioka Middle School and Agricultural High School he went climbing on Mount Iwate at least 28 times, each time examining flora and often collecting mineral specimens. Mount Iwate features frequently in his poetry and is the setting of a number of his stories, including 'The Earth God and the Fox' and 'April and the Mountain Oaf'.

There are two points of view taken in this beautiful little poem. The first depicts the mountain below, as it gouges out light from the sky. The second shows the mountain from above, its old snow (the poem carries the date 27 June 1922) deposited at the bottom of light, that is, dug into the ground.

The 'dispersed reflection' represents a scientific observation, as does the reference to a 'particle series of light'. But the word *mijin* ('particle') also has religious connotations. In Nichiren Buddhism, the expression *daichi mijin* ('dust particles of the land') is used to refer to the notion of a countless number. This expression can refer to eternal time, the incalculable number of Bodhisattvas, or even the myriad slanderers in this world.

An Impression (75)

The Larix referred to in 'An Impression', which carries the date 27 June 1922, is the deciduous larch tree that is found in Europe, North America, and Asia. In Japan it is called *karamatsu*.

Kenji is telling us in this poem that when we see a colour in nature, the colour that we see depends not only on the actual nature of the object giving it off, but also on our own mental state. That is why he referred to his poems as 'mental sketches'. In this case the thing giving off the colour is young leaves.

The colour is so intense in his mind that the 'gentleman in the observation car' (no doubt Kenji himself) is also blue, though here dark or navy blue.

'The mountain of light' referred to is Mount Iwate.

The Swordsmen's Dance of Haratai (76)

In September 1917, Kenji visited Haratai Village with fellow students on a geology excursion. He was a third-year student at Morioka Agricultural High School. At night they saw the village festival at the local shrine, surrounded by enormous cryptomeria trees. Bonfires were lit, and the village children, decked in masks and theatrical outfits, danced the same energetic dance that their ancestors had been doing for centuries. Kenji was very taken by the sound and rhythm of the drums, enough to include them in the poem as *dad-dah-dah-sko-dah-dah*. The poem carries the date 31 August 1922, five years after the excursion.

Alpen (alpine) farming refers to farming in mountainous regions.

The linden tree is the sacred bo tree beneath which the Buddha sat.

Serpentine is a metamorphic rock that is a dull green, like the colour of a snake's skin. Mount Hayachine, the tallest of the Kitakami Mountains in Iwate Prefecture, contains serpentine.

King Akuro is another name of Aterui, the great leader of the Isawa people in what is now the Tohoku region. The characters used to write the name *Akuro* mean, literally, 'bad road'.

The Lion is the constellation of Leo, visible in the night sky at the time of the festival.

To Kenji, the dance was a celebration of the human spirit and the human life that can be transformed in the time it takes a spark to shoot into the sky.

Pine Needles (78)

This is one of a number of poems written about the death of his little sister, Toshi. Toshi first became seriously ill in 1918, but did not leave her position teaching English at Hanamaki Girls School until 1921. After that, her condition worsened considerably, and Kenji returned to Hanamaki from Tokyo, to help look after her.

Kenji expresses a certain guilt here at being healthy and able to walk in the woods while his sister is burning with fever. He knows that she must take the journey after death alone, yet he begs her to take him with her.

The use of 'heavens' in the third line from the end is a play on words that exists in the original. Kenji uses *sora*, which means both 'the sky' and 'Look!'

The terpene in the second-to-last line is the hydrocarbon that occurs in the oil found in certain pines.

This poem, like 'The Morning of Last Farewell' that follows here, carries the date 27 November 1922, the day of Toshi's death. It goes without saying that they were written later and given this date for symbolic reasons.

The Morning of Last Farewell (79)

Except for the final poem in this collection, 'Strong in the Rain', this is perhaps Kenji's most famous poem. Many Japanese can quote the first two lines.

It describes the scene at Toshi's deathbed. It is sleeting outside, and yet she is burning up. She asks him to fetch her some snow. This request is made in dialect, as siblings will speak their native dialect to each other; and the last word, which implores Kenji to fetch the snow, *kenja*, can also be taken for his name, giving the line a greater poignancy.

The word for 'sloshing' is *bichobicho*, which is mimetic for sloshing or splashing.

The chipped bowl with blue watershield (*junsai*) pattern is another poignant image. This is an everyday object that brother and sister would have shared for years at their childhood home. The watershield is an aquatic plant. It is also found in North America, where it is considered a weed. But in Japan, when taken young from ponds or marshes, watershield is consumed, particularly in clear soups.

For Toshi, the sleet in the bowl soothes. To Kenji it is sent from the sky and beyond, and is a link to the place where he believes she is destined. The sky is disarranged and terrifying, because this is the place through which she must go when she passes on. But the snow is pure white, 'no matter where you take it from'. This is the absolute purity of paradise.

If Toshi eats the snow in the bowl and it enters her body, then it will, together with her body, be transformed into heaven's ice cream. Perhaps it will fall again on the earth, proving that in the pure snow is the continuing existence of Toshi Miyazawa.

Kenji stakes his happiness on his belief that the snow and her body are holy offerings to be shared in time by everyone.

Burning Desire's Past (81)

It is autumn, the rain has let up, and Kenji has gone out to transplant acacias. The poem carries the date 15 October 1923. But Kenji is a scientist who is ever distracted by his fertile imagination and by his faith. Here he sees himself as a 'transmigrating puritan' (he uses the English word 'puritan'). Transmigrating is similar to what he is about to do to the acacias. But it is more precisely a term that indicates moving from one state of existence to another. This gives the poem a Buddhist significance: that everything is evanescent, moving on in an endless cycle. (In the middle of the poem he refers to this in terms of 'a lack of dependability').

Kenji first digs a circle around the plants for transplanting. This is called *nemawashi* in Japanese. Incidentally, this word also means 'to lay the groundwork' in a metaphorical sense, and has gone into English usage, since the 1980s, as a result of the successful Japanese economic practice of building a consensus before making a decision.

Kenji is distracted by the droplets of rain or dew on the leaves of the young pear trees. In what may be the most literal display in his poems of his love of nature, he kisses the droplets, in which he sees all nature reflected (they are a kind of monad in his eyes). He even sees himself objectively as a villain, rogue, or scoundrel. There is a touch of ironic and self-deprecating humour in this self-portrait. He suspects that the acacia will be jealous of the affection he gives the pear tree. When he is finished, the droplets are gone, either fallen to the ground or evaporated.

There is an ambiguity in the title itself, in the use of *joen* ('burning desire') and *kako* ('the past'). On the one hand, the desire has become part of the past. On the other, the past itself is made up of burning desires, desires that fade, in good time, to light blue.

The Sun Sheds Slivers of Topaz (82)

This poem, which carries the date 18 May 1924, is Kenji's vision of the transition between this world and that. The clouds have congealed, rancid, in the sky. The sky itself seems to be an ocean (the larks 'rise and fall', but the word that Kenji uses also means 'to ebb and flow'). The water in the marsh itself is mercury.

The spirits of departed souls that reside in ancient trees in the Ainu legends are shaken by a wind that is balmy or fragrant (*kanbashii*). These spirits are called *kishin*, or *kijin*. They are mentioned in 'The Swordsmen's Dance of Haratai', but I have chosen to translate them there as demons, which, like 'spirits', is another meaning for this word. Departed souls or ghosts can be transformed into demons or angry gods.

The wind is a very common element in Kenji's poems and stories, and it can be seen as a medium of transmigration. Once spirits are freed, they can roam: the moth is released and crosses over the sprouting swamp cabbage.

I have taken liberty in the translation of the plant that I have called 'swamp cabbage'. The original is *mizubasho*, a word that sounds beautiful in Japanese and that coincidentally contains the name of the famous haiku poet Basho. The correct English translation of *mizubasho* is 'skunk cabbage', and it grows commonly in the western wetlands of North America. I just couldn't bring myself to be correct here, and chose sound and imagery over the literal.

The *mizubasho* sprouts in early spring; and while the American *mizubasho* has a foul smell, hence its name, in Japan the plant smells much less offensive, something like grease. It appears in Ainu legend and is called, in the Ainu language, *usis kina*.

True to Kenji's view of life, the moth crosses over and beyond, but the sprouts themselves are a sign of new life. All new life and departing life are bound together, and Kenji always sees the clearest evidence of this in spring.

The Tsugaru Strait (83)

The Tsugaru Strait lies between Japan's main island of Honshu and the northern island of Hokkaido. In Kenji's time, Japan stretched further north than Hokkaido up to Sakhalin.

Kenji wrote a number of poems about his sister's death, believing that he could communicate with her on his trips to the far north. This poem is a kind of introduction to the others. He has just started out on his journey.

There are two poems with this title. The earlier one carries the date 1 August 1923; this one, dated 19 May 1924 is, to my mind, the far better poem. Some of Kenji's longer poems are rambling. There are admirers of his poems who are drawn to these. After all, Kenji walks about outside and records what he observes. When he reworked a poem, however, and made it more concise, as he clearly did with this one, I cannot help but feel that he intended to create something definitive. This later version is also supported by an earlier draft subtitled 'Water Marriage'.

It is this water marriage that is the theme. The two great peninsulas that jut north off Honshu – the Tsugaru and Shimokita Peninsulas – are linked by the raging sea (Kenji does love his storms!).

119

The result is 'a flashy and lucid wedding'.

'Tin pest', or 'tin disease', is a term used to describe the disintegration of shiny tin into a grey powder that crumbles. It is a startling image for these dark clouds rimmed by the sun.

'Arsenic mirror' represents a method for detecting the presence of arsenic, by heating arsenious oxide to form a black deposit that resembles a mirror.

Kenji is very familiar with the scientific procedures associated with terms like tin pest and arsenic mirror.

After the space in the lines, which indicates the passage of time, the ferry approaches Hokkaido, and the land undulates under the sun and the whirling black tails of the clouds. It is almost as if he feels he is about to enter another world.

The Petals of Karma (84)

The teachings of Nichiren Buddhism, to which Kenji adhered to ardently, are based on the Lotus Sutra, and the petals in this poem belong to the lotus flower.

In Kenji's more desolate moments – and they were many – he grieved over the 'bad karma' in him, depicted here as dark petals. He didn't see himself as a describer of nature, but rather as its recorder or chronicler, faithfully writing down entries in nature's diary day after day. This poem carries the date 5 October 1924.

An Icy Joke (85)

Kenji Miyazawa was a deeply serious and excessively earnest person – not to mention a diligent and obsessive worker – but he did have his lighter side. This shows up in his stories and plays more than in his poems.

His sense of humour took a number of forms. His humour is evident in the plays that he wrote for the farmers in the districts around Hanamaki. He saw these plays as a tool to teach morality to them. The style of this humour can probably be best described as 'straightforward and rustic'.

The comic touches in his stories are innocent. His sense of humour in them is usually childlike. Most adults in Kenji's stories are portrayed from the standpoint of children, and their gestures, traits, and foibles often appear comic as a result. There is some black humour in Kenji, too, as in his story 'The Restaurant of Many Orders,' where two hunters find that the dining tables have turned on them.

But rarely would Kenji's humour be called worldly or sophisticated, and there is little cynicism in him. 'An Icy Joke' is an exception. The cutting irony in this poem, which carries the date 18 January 1925, comes from animosity, in this case animosity aimed at a colleague of his at Hanamaki Agricultural School named Shirafuji. Shirafuji is barely disguised here as Shirabuchi. This poem is an out-and-out polemic against what Kenji saw as a sham religious belief. Thirty-nine degrees north latitude is where Hanamaki is located, making it quite clear where this 'joke' is meant to take place.

What has happened to Hanamaki? It has found itself inside a desert. Kenji uses the word *sunakemuri*, which in this scene of desertification, is a 'cloud of fine sand'. Kenji's modifying of this with 'frozen' is a good example of his phenomenology, where hot and cold often merge, as do solid, liquid, and gas.

The *nemu*, or silk tree, blooms in summer (*nemu* has a beautiful sound in Japanese, similar to *nemuru*, the word for 'to sleep'). Its flowers are associated in Kenji's northern district with the stars, particularly in connection with the Tanabata legend, according to which two stars (Altair and Vega) represent long-lost lovers, separated by the Milky Way, who are able to meet just once a year, on 7 July.

Kenji jumps, as he so often does, from the lyrical to the mundane, with the latter represented here in the form of term schedules for school. He interjects colloquial language: 'That's right...there's no doubt about it.'

His use of 'virtual' is both poetic and technical, as, for instance, its use as a term in optics. Here it is a ghost image, as opposed to a real image of an object. The exotic atmosphere is accentuated by camels and caravans. But we find that as we go north the journey takes us from stifling heat to the polar sea. Kenji is constantly telling us that we can be transformed in what appears as an instant, that life is but a fleeting moment, and that true salvation can be had in another realm. And so, heat turns to cold; water to ice; mountains crumble; rivers are diverted; light and air become media of change.

The white lily is associated in India with the search for true happiness, and this is what Kenji has in mind when he introduces it. The white lily is the symbol of the Women's Division of the Soka Gakkai, the largest Nichiren Buddhist organisation in Japan today.

Gatha is the Sanskrit word for verse or hymn. Some *gathas* come in couplets, others are longer. Which gatha did Kenji have in mind? Perhaps it was this one from the Five Remembrances, which he knew.

> All that is dear to me and everyone that I love are of the nature of change
> There is no way to escape being separated from them

January on the Iwate Light Railway (86)

The Iwate Light Railway, which no longer exists, was among a considerable number of narrow gauge (762mm) lines built in Japan. It is said that this railway was the model for the Milky Way train.

This poem describes a scene during the coldest season in the north and carries the date 17 January 1926. In January snow falls in Iwate on an average of 26 days.

Each tree that the train passes is given its common name and its Latin one, Kenji adding the suffix '-lander' to the latter. The origin of this suffix is unknown, but it apparently stood in his mind for plants or trees growing on the embankment of a river, so I have translated it with 'Riverlander'.

The Light Pole Grande of Hanamaki, or *hanamaki grande denchu*, was a column of tall light poles, with clusters of glass insulators, outside Hanamaki. In the imaginary name that Kenji gave to this column of poles, he envisaged them as cavalry, as indicated by the use of *fusa* ('tasselled'). This connects with the word 'column' at the end of the poem.

In the line about Alnus Riverlander, the word 'mirror' appears four times, together, as if forming one word. The original has the character for 'mirror' together in a cluster of four. Here Kenji is painting a picture of the ribbonlike staminate flowers of the black alder that hang from the branches during this season. The 'mirrors' that appear in this poem are made from the steam that comes from the train and freezes on the branches of the various trees.

Kenji is on his train as it travels north. When he finally comes to the mulberry tree, the wind caused by the train's motion sends 'icy flowers' sailing through the air, as if in response to his wishes. It is a coincidence – and one that Kenji would have appreciated – that in English 'light railway' has two distinct meanings.

High Grade Mist (87)

This is an early summer farmyard scene, filled with so much light that it is almost blinding. Kenji uses the English word 'high grade' to describe the mist caught in blaring light in this poem, which carries the date 27 June 1922.

Cloud Signal (88)

'Cloud Signal' carries the date 10 May 1922.

Kenji here sees meaning in the clouds of spring. The pale spring sky is attesting to the virtue of self-denial. There is no doubt that self-denial here refers not to modesty, but to the suppression of human desire and greed. This is a poem about faith as illustrated by something in nature.

The four cryptomeria are actually a so-named row of four of these trees in Hanamaki. Unfortunately they were chopped down some years ago. It is ironical at best that now, with Kenji its most famous son, the city of Hanamaki has erected four little concrete pillars by the side of the road in the spot where these trees stood in Kenji's day.

A Report (89)

Kenji is fond of formal statements-as-poems such as 'A Report,' which carries the date 15 June 1922.

This one may appear to be a product of his very fertile imagination. Apparently, however, there was just such a rainbow seen in the district that afternoon. In addition, as is rare with rainbows, it remained in the sky for an hour from about 3:20 P.M., relatively low over the horizon. The upper part of this rainbow, it is said, glowed red against the distant hills.

Kenji was just recording what he saw.

Clearing (90)

'Clearing,' which carries the date 27 March 1927, is a rather unusual poem for Kenji in that it depicts him working intimately with other people. In this poem, he and others are clearing the land for cultivation, as the title in Japanese, *kaikon*, suggests. Totally exhausted, they collapse into the bamboo grass and snore away.

The amazing images of the last two lines are either dreams or a record of things actually occurring nearby. The needles here are a metaphor for light on the water. As for herons, they appear notably in *Night on the Milky Way Train* as migrating through the heavens.

This concise poem combines Kenji's down-to-earth working life with his vision of the next world.

Romance (91)

This poem, which carries the date 2 April 1927, appears to be an unusual one for Kenji. But when one considers that the 'boy' and 'girl' here are frogs, and that this romance has religious overtones, it is well in line with his views on nature, faith, and love.

The setting is idyllic, with its apple tree and rose-coloured sky. The town's illumination has the quality of gelatinous agar: Kenji's metaphors are often based on a thing having the consistency or properties of something else, particularly a denser substance. The Japanese word for agar is *kanten*, which is written with the characters for 'cold sky'. (Agar, or agar-agar, is a very common substance and food in Japan. Though it was first used to culture bacteria by Robert Koch in the 1880s, the Japanese soon developed a virtual monopoly on its manufacture. In Kenji's day, most of the agar used in the world came from Japan.)

The 'Keolg Kol' and 'Keolg Kohl' are mimetic croaking sounds that appear exactly like this in Roman letters in the original. It is the way the frogs' croaking sounded to Kenji at the time.

The 'black cloak' is night, and the blue halo is a symbol of the life beyond this one. This boy frog and girl frog *know* where they are destined, and it is that conviction that gives rise to their devotion to one another.

Strong in the Rain (92)

Kenji's best-known poem remained unpublished in his lifetime. It had been written in his little notebook with the title 'November 3' and discovered after his death. In this poem Kenji gives us a portrait of his ideal life. The 3 November is 1931, less than two years before he died. He wrote his will shortly before writing this poem. Perhaps he saw the poem as a kind of prayerful wish for himself in his next life.

Kenji desperately desired to have a strong, robust and healthy body. Needless to say, this is a wish that is common to all people. But Kenji's desire for this contained a motivation that most of us would not claim for ourselves. Like the scorpion in *Night on the Milky Way Train* that burns its body to provide light and heat, Kenji wanted to use his body for the good of humanity. If you are sickly and weak, what sacrifices can you make for all of the humans who need you?

Kenji was utterly sincere in his wish to suppress and stifle his natural desires. These included natural physical drives such as those for food and sex, as well as material desires, such as those for wealth and comfort. Because of the asceticism inspired in him by his religion, Kenji denied himself these desires. To him, love meant only devotion and sacrifice. One's body must be robust, never sidetracked by worldly desires. The body, like the mind, must always be equal to the task of fulfilling its occupant's holy mission.

His last request to his father, on the morning of 21 September 1933 – he died at 1.30 P.M. that same day – was to print up a thousand copies of the Lotus Sutra to distribute to his friends and acquaintances.

Author, playwright, theatre director and translator, **Roger Pulvers** has published 30 books in English and Japanese, including novels, plays, collected essays, translations (from Japanese, Russian and Polish), and his autobiography, *The Unmaking of an American*. His most recent book is *The Honey and the Fires* (ABC Books, Australia), secular stories from the Bible rewritten for the 21st century.